"Joy's wisdom will open your heart and guide you to the luminous inspiration of your soul. If you want to awaken, read this book!"

~ **Ana Holub**, author of *Forgive and Be Free*

"Joy can show you how to bring spirituality to everyday life."

~ **Peter Mt. Shasta**, author of *Adventures of a Western Mystic I and II*

INSPIRED

INSPIRED

7 Wisdoms of a Soul Inspired Life

By Joy Taylor

LIFESTYLE
ENTREPRENEURS
PRESS
LAS VEGAS, NV

ISBN: 978-1-948-78717-8
Published by
Lifestyle Entrepreneurs Press
Las Vegas, NV

If you are interested in publishing through Lifestyle Entrepreneurs Press, write to: *Publishing@LifestyleEntrepreneursPress.com*

Publications or foreign rights acquisitions of our catalog books. Learn More: *www.LifestyleEntrepreneursPress.com*

Printed in the USA

Illustrations and Poetry by Joy Taylor
Book cover design by Debbie o'Bryne, *https://JetLaunch.com*

To Nonnie (my grandma) and Auntie (my great-aunt) —
Two brave souls who found peace within,
Your legacies of love live on and on.

Table of Contents

INSPIRED

Foreword to
INSPIRED: 7 Wisdoms of a Soul Inspired Life

By Marci Shimoff

Too often, when I ask people how they're doing, they respond with something like, "I'm okay. I'm getting by. I'm surviving."

This breaks my heart. I don't believe we're put on this planet to just survive. We're here to *thrive*. But in order to do that, we have to connect with our soul, which guides us to live an inspired life. That soul connection gives us the clarity to see what we're really here to do in this world—what our purpose and calling is.

In my years of research on lasting happiness, I've found that living an inspired life is one of the essential keys to deep fulfillment. The happiest people are those who are "lit up" and overflowing with passion and purpose.

I first witnessed the magic of living with purpose in my father, a deeply happy man who lived a completely inspired life. Every day, he loved going to work as a dentist. When he retired, I worried about him because I'd read the research showing how people's health often declines dramatically after they retire because they lose their sense of purpose. Not my dad. He vowed, "That's not going to happen to me. I'm going to stay inspired."

To find out what really lit his fire, he analyzed what he loved about being a dentist. It turned out that what brought him joy was working with his hands in intricate ways. For him, dentistry was artwork. So, at age seventy-two, he began his second "profession"—needlepoint. He became a master needle-pointer and won awards throughout California into his late eighties. Every morning at 9:00 a.m., he would go to his needlepoint office (my sister's old bedroom), put on his dental magnifying glasses, and begin his work. He was in heaven creating exquisite art on fabric, and he left a beautiful legacy for my siblings and me in both his artwork and in his example of inspired living.

We each can live an inspired life! No matter what talents you possess, what stage of life you're in, or what your past experiences have been, you *can* live filled with purpose. And this book will show you how.

I believe in *Inspired* for two reasons:

First, I know in my heart that nothing is more important than living a life aligned with your soul's inspiration. It's essential not only for your own personal happiness, but also for a better world. Imagine what our planet would look like if everyone was living a soul inspired life.

Second, I believe in this book because I believe in Joy Taylor. She's an emphatic "Yes!" for the highest and best for every person. She is generous, creative, open-hearted, and filled with integrity. Joy lives this message every day, as inspiration is her calling and her authentic gift.

If you're ready to embrace a deeply meaningful and love-filled life, this book is your golden ticket. It offers you the tools to live as the joyful person you were born to be. By opening up to the wisdom on these pages, you're making an empowered choice to stop settling for "just surviving." You're choosing to connect with your inspiration, stand in your unique brilliance, and fully thrive.

There is no better time to begin than now. As Howard Thurman eloquently said, "Don't ask yourself what the world needs. Ask yourself what makes you come alive, and then go do that. Because what the world needs are people who have come alive."

Thank you, Joy, for bringing your accessible, life-inspiring wisdom to the world. And thank you, Reader, for opening your heart to receive this message.

May we all live fully alive, together.

With love,

Marci Shimoff
San Anselmo, California
March, 2019

INTRODUCTION

The Wisdoms

"Putting love first means knowing the Universe supports you in creating the good, the holy, and the beautiful. It means knowing you're on the earth for a purpose, and that the purpose itself will create opportunities for its accomplishment."

—MARIANNE WILLIAMSON

American Spiritual Teacher, Author, and Lecturer

Have you been yearning to live a more inspired life? One that ignites your purpose? One that catalyzes courage and self-esteem? One that makes you feel joy? I believe we all want to live a life that makes a difference, a life that gives back to the world creatively and with heart.

My journey of stepping into a purposeful life began when I was a child. At five, I received a bright idea and changed my name from Jo to Joy. I believe that change set in motion a resonance that has uplifted me ever since. As a young adult, I followed the promptings of a vision that led me to the base of a mountain, which became a nurturing home for twenty years. Just before I turned forty, I heard a voice in the high desert that guided me to pivot in my vocation in order to fulfill a higher potential.

I followed these inner promptings. I trusted them. Something deep inside of me responded with a resounding "yes." In every case, life only got better. You might have a few stories like that too. You might have had a hunch, an "aha" moment, or a lightning bolt experience that inspired you to make a shift and it turned out to be positive. You also may have had some promptings that you ignored—and you regretted it. These benevolent inner promptings may come to you in random, unpredictable ways, but they can have a profound effect on you when you obey their messages.

A Messenger of Inspiration

I was reinventing my training company's mission statement back in 2012, and I wanted to hone in on a clear focus. After fourteen years of teaching wellness and business, I went directly to my clients for input on a renewed purpose, and a pivot in what and how I trained. The responses were telling and a central theme emerged: people felt that they were changing through the power of inspiration. They saw me as a messenger of that positive force.

Taking my clients' comments as my lead, I started posting more about inspiration. I blogged on it, offered social shares, interviewed people, and researched the topic of inspiration. I consulted my inner knowing and stretched my understanding of this profound concept. I started presenting a signature talk, *The Power of Inspiration*, for various audiences, especially business events and women's leadership groups. People were craving it! And loving it. I applied inspiration to marketing and business planning through mission, vision, and values statements. I brought inspiration to my work with clients and companies.

In my research, I asked questions like, "What is the deeper meaning of *inspiration*? How can we live more inspired lives?

What nurtures inspiration? Are some people naturally born to inspire?" The answers I found, along with many real-life illustrations, are included in the pages that follow. In my investigations, I realized that within the most profound and awesome creative expressions, accomplishments, and activities, inspiration is at work—guiding and propelling humanity forward, moving through us, and as us, when we allow it. At our best we are the vessels of inspiration.

"Within the most profound and awesome creative expressions, accomplishments, and activities, inspiration is at work— guiding and propelling humanity forward, moving through us, and as us, when we allow it."

The traditional definition of *inspiration* is the process of being mentally stimulated to do or feel something, especially to do something creative.

However, inspiration also means to *breathe in*. The process of breathing is divided into two distinct phases, inspiration (inhalation) and expression (exhalation.) When I share this definition during live presentations, I invite participants to stand up and take deep breaths in-and-out. I invite people to visualize energy streaming into their body with each breath. I'm inviting you to do the same. Wherever you are, take a deep breath. Try it. Slow breathing will relax you. Fast breathing may excite you.

Conscious deep breathing as a tool, is an automatic way to be inspired. Inhale—you are inspiring yourself, literally. Deep breathing is renewing, stimulating, calming, and oxygenating. I highly recommend a practice of breathing and/or breath-work therapies as a fast track to an inspired life. Take a few more glorious breaths. Enjoy the miracle of life.

Now that you are likely feeling more centered, inhale again and hold your breath. Hold your breath for as long as you can. How does that feel? It is painful, right? Keep on holding your breath until you just cannot hold it any longer. Holding? Okay... let it go. Exhale and release.

Like holding your breath, inspiration without expression is painful. This exercise illustrates that inspiration is the precursor to expression. It is a natural rhythm. Within our unique lives, if we feel inspired and don't act on it, we slowly die in spirit, just like we would die in form without the balance of inhalation and exhalation.

Maya Angelou states, "There is no greater agony than bearing an untold story inside you." Your breath, your inspiration, your passion is your story, and there are people in this world who want to hear your story. No doubt about it. We want your story, your song, and your unique expressions.

What I now know is that inspiration will take you where you want to go. It will provide more pleasure and peace than you could have imagined. It will show up in ways better than what you have dreamed and more playfully than your mind could have directed. But the kind of inspiration that comes directly from your soul center requires a paradigm shift in how you see the world and yourself. Indeed, the path of soul inspiration is right in front of us, but so few of us see it. Even fewer act on it.

"Inspiration will take you where you want to go."

Soul Inspired People are:

- Guiding Lights
- Truth Tellers
- Mentors and Teachers
- Catalysts for Positive Change
- Leaders of a Better World
- Humble Volunteers
- Healers in Their Presence
- Honest Friends
- Pioneers of Consciousness
- Artists of Life

The Journey

This book takes you on a journey to living a soul inspired life, a life where your soul, not your personality, leads the way. As Gary Zukav, author of *Seat of the Soul* states, "When the personality comes to serve the energy of your soul, that is authentic power." Instead of being controlled by the desires and fears of your personality, you utilize the gifts and talents of your personality and fulfill your purpose. Instead of seeking external power, you find your strength within.

A soul inspired life is not about acquiring; it's about receiving. It's not about making things happen; it's about allowing things to happen. It's not about changing on the outside; it's about transforming on the inside. It's about getting intimate with all your feelings—yes, that means the pain, fear, shame, and anger that reside within you as well as the joy, love, and compassion. It's about the courage to see your own light and shine it, to co-creatively dance with your destiny.

If you are open and willing, the teachings in the pages that follow can change you—perhaps even drastically transform your life. You may gain the fortitude to follow a dream, speak up, forgive, open your heart for deeper intimacy, or find more compatible and supportive relationships. You might start new health habits or let go of an addiction. But change happens only if, as you read, you utilize not only your mental capacities but employ your intuitive and spiritual nature as well—for embodied learning involves all of you. I invite you to put your heart front and center. I invite you to know your shadows and be freed from their hold on your life.

If you choose, you will cut the binds that hold you back, unleashing yourself from self-imposed restraints. You will come to know fear as a call to trust. You will see a more expanded view of your circumstances, including seeing your previous blind spots. This is great insight! I'm encouraging you to give up victimhood. As you rest in your empowered self, you will take responsibility for all of you—what you like and what you hide. I'm welcoming you to both fall back and leap forward as we journey together. Wherever you are, it is the perfect place to be. When you realize that life is unfolding as it is meant to—life becomes more fun.

As business executive Stephanie Hoffman says, "The true measure of knowing if you are in the right work, right relationship, or even correct purpose in life is if you can whole-heartedly say, 'I like who I am becoming.'" Life is about becoming. This book is about becoming—becoming a soul inspired version of you, the one you were born to be.

Transform with Wisdom

I discovered the Seven Wisdoms through a series of promptings and found them to be the keys for creating a purposeful life.

These are the fundamental principles that I live by. I believe these Wisdoms are essential to feeling supported, connected, and loved. I believe these Wisdoms give you the courage and guidance to share your glorious innate gifts. When adopted and acted upon, the Seven Wisdoms enlighten your life's journey, bringing grace and greater fulfillment. If you employ these Wisdoms, you will find confidence, inner strength, and more meaning in your life. Life still throws curve balls, but you are equipped to respond (whether you catch or dodge them).

I received an introduction to these Wisdoms one morning after a cup of coffee and a contemplative prayer. They came to me as a blessing. First, I heard an inner voice that said, "Life is for you." Stunned by the simple clarity, I took out my iPhone and made a note. Then I heard, "You deserve good." Once again, I made a note of the statement. I pondered, if life is for me and I deserve the good that comes to me, then I must learn

to trust life's cues. The message that followed was, "Life will prompt you." This series of statements established the first three

Wisdoms. From there, four more distinct statements came forth: "I will have the courage to take action on these promptings. I will learn from each experience. I am grateful for my life. I choose to serve."

Over time, I developed the Seven Wisdoms into solid, usable, and transformative ideals. I practiced them, and I found beneficial results. So did friends, clients, and family members. I enthusiastically recommend you do the same. Eventually, when practiced, the Seven Wisdoms can empower you to live life with clear purpose and intention, to know your true essence, and to make conscious decisions from that place. The Wisdoms apply to work situations, relationships, and health. They allow us to live, love, and lead soul inspired lives.

Soul Inspired Presence

There is something beyond our physical selves. You can think of that something as pure energy. Often, it is called Spirit. This magnificent energy elicits awe and feels like beauty: One feels humbled in its Presence. While this mysterious wonder is indescribable, it goes by many names: Creative Intelligence, The Unified Field, Source, Divine, God, Oneness, or the Universe.

A part of that pure energy is the individual soul. Your soul is a spark of the Divine that expresses itself through you and as you. Like a drop of water in an ocean, your soul is a drop of Spirit.

Your soul is infinite. It is that which you were before you were born and that which you will be after your body dies. When you live aligned with your soul, connected to Spirit, you employ the physical, emotional, and mental aspects of yourself to serve the good. Your soul infuses your personality.

To orient yourself as a soul is to gain a larger picture of life and a far more objective view of yourself, the world, and other living beings. You come to realize that you are connected to all that is.

This broader perspective allows you to:
- Examine aspects of yourself that interfere with you expressing your soul essence.
- Question limiting assumptions and paradigms you have lived by.
- Transform low self-esteem into self-compassion and love.

As Russian novelist Leo Tolstoy wrote, "Everyone thinks of changing the world, but no one thinks of changing himself." Soul inspired people start with changing themselves, and the world benefits as a result—in immeasurable ways.

Please note: To be soul inspired is not to be exaggerated in unfounded optimism. For the truth of our being lies in the shadow as much as the light. Indeed, we are after a wholeness that encourages full investigation of all our experiences. We become liberated and reunited with our soul when we give up denial and become intimate with all that we feel.

This book is not about spiritual bypass, it is about an inclusive way of being on planet Earth—with your soul in the lead. It is about self-awareness, inner-honoring, and pioneering change! When you are devoted to your authentic purpose, what you want, wants you.

"When you are devoted to your authentic purpose, what you want, wants you."

In a soul inspired life, you remember that you entered the world as love and realize your true essence as love. You choose to be mindful and caring through your thoughts, words, and actions. You make insightful choices based on your soul's knowing, which ultimately lead to positive results for you and others and to feelings of well-being. A soul inspired life is a creative life, a happy life, a life of service without the need to prove or please.

A soul inspired life is a life with mutually rewarding relationships. It is a life that renews you with energy. Your work is infused with meaning and your innovative impulses take flight. The Seven Wisdoms and the companion exercises offered in this book give you the opportunity to embody inspiration to live in Spirit.

Beginning with the first Wisdom, you come to understand that you live in a Benevolent Universe, and you embrace the idea that the Universe is for you, that life is on your side. The next Wisdoms build upon this knowing, with the final Wisdoms inviting you to give back to others with gratitude for what you have received.

Perhaps you haven't taken the time to consider how your feelings and behaviors might be affecting your life. Perhaps you have and are ready to go deeper and to clear out more of the interference of negative thinking and feeling. Are you aware of the particular emotions or thoughts that dictate your actions?

Quantum physicists tell us that our thinking governs our world. Neuroscientists conclude that our thinking is, to a large part, controlled by a conditioned subconscious mind. It is time to rethink our thinking, and this book will help you do that.

By reading the descriptions of the Wisdoms and the stories that illustrate them, you will see that your world reflects your current inner landscape and thoughts. This affords you considerable personal power in navigating situations and circumstances. With awareness comes conscious choice.

So, ask yourself: Do you like the reflection you are seeing? Conversely, do you feel trapped or unfulfilled?

- Are you feeling exhausted because you care-take others at the expense of you?
- Are you yearning for freedom but perpetually choose what is safe instead?
- Are you doubting your ability to accomplish your big dreams?
- Are you holding back from intimate love?
- Are you letting logic lead instead of your heart?

If you answered "yes" to any of these questions, or if you have a sense that there might be a more rewarding or destined path for you, perhaps now is the time to make a change. If you are willing, this book will introduce you to a new way of being, working, loving, and visioning, where you can live congruent with your values. Just imagine what life could be like if you gave up the need to please or to prove yourself. Imagine designing your destiny, instead of living by default.

Patañjali, who compiled the Yoga Sutras of India, wrote, "When you are inspired by some great purpose, some extraordinary project, all your thoughts break their bonds: Your mind transcends limitations, your consciousness expands in every direction, and you find yourself in a new, great, and wonderful world. Dormant forces, faculties, and talents become alive, and you discover yourself to be a greater person by far than you ever dreamed yourself to be."

The Rewards of a Soul Inspired Life

As you get into the practice of living with a soulful orientation, you'll find that fears fall away. The fears of failure and rejection will diminish. Even fears such as public speaking, falling in love, or launching a new business will no longer limit or control you.

When you live a soul inspired life, you place inner peace ahead of how you appear in the world. You care more about your soul inspired ideals than your physical identity, your history, or the perceptions of others. Boldly, you acquire the tools and fortitude to face your shadows, the parts of you that you have previously denied or disowned. You might begin to face them like the visiting guests in Rumi's poem "The Guest House," understanding that "your sorrows may be clearing you out for some new delight."

Perhaps one of the most well-known examples of someone who lives a soul inspired life is businesswoman, talk show host, actress, producer, and philanthropist, Oprah Winfrey. Oprah transcended a tumultuous childhood to become one of the most influential and powerful women in the world. She uses her media presence and network, her fame, and her fortune to improve the welfare of people and humanitarian causes around the world.

As Oprah demonstrates, when you live a soul inspired life, your measures of success shift from personal accolades, material accumulations, and trophy-like accomplishments to caring about others and contributing to the greater good. That is not to say that you give up achievement or material possessions. In fact, like Oprah, you may find yourself surrounded with more abundance than you ever dreamed possible, but deep down you know where your real treasures lie. Soul inspired leaders naturally move forward with a cause and others follow. Humbly, these leaders stay steady towards their philanthropic vision, keenly aware that the process must be congruent with the outcome. In soul inspired business, the triple bottom line is people, planet, and profit. In soul inspired relationships, we establish compassionate and connected ways of being together for the purpose of growth. A soul inspired attitude and approach touches every area of life.

When you are soul inspired, you:
- Realize that you are more than your body, personality, mind, and the conditioned beliefs that may have ruled you.
- Understand that your true purpose extends far beyond your work, roles, or financial status.
- Align with your gifts and your values, and let life use you for a greater good.

As you live a soul inspired life, you can expect that you will receive many blessings without manipulating your gains. It is a life of wonder and surprise.

If you are disappointed in life, inspiration can feel like a demand from an authoritative parent. The idea (or threat) of inspiration can make you want to hide under your covers or to shout out and rebel. You run to safe addictions, like electronics, social media, eating, drinking, shopping, or entertainment—like romantic movies and novels—anything to evade change. The inner critic who lives inside of your mind, might tell you false stories such as, "You're not good enough. You won't amount to anything. Stay safe."

When we avoid inspiration's call, friends with the same addictions or tendencies are a comfort. We share the same social standards, feel good about our common complacency, and hide within a tribe that is also living an uninspired, safe life. The inertia of safe and stuck can be temporary; or, if you don't make a leap of faith, it can become a habit that lasts a lifetime. Why? Because a numb, secure way of living is acceptable in our culture, and frankly, it can be easy. But if you are reading this book, you are already considering that you want to take the leap.

Introducing the Seven Wisdoms

The Seven Wisdoms are the wind under your wings. They are truths that give unwavering security and comfort when times are hard, when you face doubt, or when you're stuck. They can keep you on track to live empowered and heart-centered. They keep you from succumbing to confusion, distractions, and unhealthy habits.

The Seven Wisdoms provide a way to be aware and fearless in this often murky and mysterious world, while deliberately co-creating your life and accepting your role in it. Unfounded fears, that do not threaten your life or survival, are seen as false and are released—not followed. Inspiration leads the way. You follow the summons to serve, to experience conscious connection with others, and to pursue your passions.

This book presents the Seven Wisdoms in a melodic progression. In other words, the Wisdoms comfortably build upon each other like notes of a scale.

Wisdom One affirms a fundamental belief that life is for you. This has the potential to be a significant paradigm shift. Wisdom Two encourages self-compassion, self-worth, and nurturing activities, which increase receptivity to Wisdom Three, recognizing and following life's cues.

By experiencing a kinship with the first three Wisdoms, you become empowered to experience the next four. Overall, you become more certain of yourself and the choices you make. When you tap into trust, self-acceptance, and intuition, your confidence will grow, and you will be guided into new situations so that you live the life you were meant to live. Becoming powerfully authentic feels wonderful. Welcome home.

Wisdoms Four and Five demonstrate how to show up fully in the world. Wisdom Four encourages taking inspired action so you can express and create at your full potential. Wisdom Five teaches that, no matter the outcome of an experience (whether it goes your way or not), you are learning and growing, which is "a big prize" in itself. These Wisdoms give you permission to make mistakes and explore life to the fullest.

Wisdom Six asks you to give thanks for the good in your life—even the hard stuff. When you count your blessings and notice your good fortune, more good comes your way. At the highest level, you say, "Thank you, everything." Wisdom Seven is a natural outgrowth of the blessings received in the earlier Wisdoms—it is the desire to give back with whole-hearted service. Grand achievements done by one individual and multiplied by many are what can change and revolutionize the world. I hope that is what you are after: to be a change agent for a better humanity.

Your Purpose Is to Give 7

1 Life Is for You

2 You Deserve Love

Choose Gratitude 6

Soul Inspired

Life Is Guiding You 3

Learn as You Live 5

4 Take Inspired Action

Attributes, Affirmations, and Actions

In order to support you in receiving the full gift of the Seven Wisdoms, the Wisdoms are unpacked and explained with accompanying *attributes*, *affirmations*, and *actions*. When you embody the Wisdoms, you naturally feel the attributes, think the affirmations, and do the actions in harmonious resonance with your soul.

The *attributes* are characteristics, traits, and qualities you develop. The more you deeply take in, accept, and acclimate to the Wisdoms, the more you exude their qualities.

The *affirmations* are the thoughts you think as you internalize each Wisdom. These positive statements help you secure and master the mindset of each Wisdom. If you stand strong in the dynamic force of authentic belief, these words and thoughts will reshape not just your thinking but also your brain. The science of neuroplasticity has demonstrated that our brain patterns can change. We can train ourselves to rewire, to thrive. We can repattern our minds towards self-empowering thoughts, especially when we nurture natural feelings and beliefs that reflect the Wisdoms. You can learn much more about designing "Start Where You Are Affirmations" in the Appendix. (Take a peek now if you like.)

The *actions* suggest ways to experiment and practice the Seven Wisdoms. They become the evidence that you are living the Wisdoms. This is where the rubber meets the road. Believing and affirming have little power without action to back them up. Action brings the Seven Wisdoms to life in real time! The suggested activities at the end of each chapter are designed to inspire you to embody each Wisdom. Even if the actions don't seem comfortable at first, they can become authentic over time. Moving one step at a time, you will come to see that your natural inclination is to be aligned with the Benevolent Universe. Simultaneously, you'll notice that your actions shift on their own accord as you embody the truth of each Wisdom. You slowly stretch yourself into a more soul inspired you.

Wisdom Warriors

As a companion guide on your journey through the Wisdoms, I share stories from my own life and the stories of my friends, clients, colleagues, and mentors. Some names have been changed to maintain their privacy.

Through a prompting early in my life, I got the sense that I ought to listen to the people whom I admired and to follow their lead. This is why when I set new intentions or goals, like writing *Inspired,* I find knowledgeable guides who have mastered what I want to learn and I learn from them.

Throughout the book I impart the highlights of extensive research and interviews with some of my favorite spiritual teachers, whom I call Wisdom Warriors. I am especially honored to introduce my core teacher, who prefers to remain anonymous. I refer to him as David. I met him when I was twenty-three. More than two decades later, he continues to inspire and instruct me. His teachings are filtered through my memory and personal perception. I do my best to express these enlightened truths with clarity.

You will also meet my beloved, Kirk. He encourages me to choose love, not fear. In our relationship, the Wisdoms came to life through daily practice and study. We do our best to walk the talk. *Inspired* reflects these experiences.

Experiment with the Wisdoms

As you read the Seven Wisdoms, I invite you to question and evaluate the validity of each one and to ask how it pertains to your life. I offer you ways to experiment. I encourage you to study each Wisdom for yourself. You might recognize that you already live in accordance with the principles. Hone your skills and move on to the next Wisdom. If a particular Wisdom is more challenging, try it on and take more time to understand it. The more you review, the deeper you'll go.

Some questions you can ask are:
- How might this Wisdom transform my life?
- Do I exemplify the attributes? How?
- Are the affirmations congruent with my current beliefs?
- Who would I be if I believed this affirmation?
- Are my actions in accordance with this Wisdom?
- How can I apply this Wisdom?

You'll gain the most from this book if you journal, dialogue with others, and earnestly practice the Wisdoms. At the conclusion of each chapter, you'll find "Gems for the Journey," a summary section that can be a handy reference and reminder. You will also be offered concrete suggestions in the form of "Walking with the Wisdoms" that can help you embody the new truths. Engage with them. Try them on! For those of you who journal, I suggest the "Inner-Views" offered—they will prompt you towards uncovering insights through inquiry.

More resources are available at the end of the book. You might also like to visit *www.ASoulInspiredLife.com*, where you will find additional programs and gifts to enrich your understanding and experience. *The Inspired Guidebook* is available on Amazon and in bookstores.

So, let's *do* this. Are you ready? I celebrate that we are all evolving together on this beautiful Earth, which is a great place to be when you are on the path to living a soul inspired life.

This Moment

Ask me about God,
I'll tell you about the love between a man and a woman,
A child and her mother.

Ask me about Devotion,
We will dig in the soil, tend to the garden,
And watch the vegetables grow.

Ask me about Prayer,
We will make up a song that has never been sung,
Then, we will sing another.

Ask me about Service,
I will prepare you a meal,
And laugh with you through the dark night.

Ask me who my Teacher is,
I will unwrap the layers of my heart,
Until you can feel love's presence.

Ask me about Spirituality,
I will bring you right to this moment,
And you will stop asking.

WISDOM

Life Is for You

"The most important decision we make is whether we believe we live in a friendly or hostile Universe."

—ALBERT EINSTEIN
Theoretical Physicist and Creator of the Theory of Relativity

The first Wisdom on the path to a soul inspired life invites you to make a life-defining choice about how you view the Universe and your relationship to it. Your choice will set the foundation for experiencing all of what life brings your way. Will you dismiss or celebrate happy times? Will you bear or transcend hardships? Will you trust that your life circumstances are in accordance with your best interests? As Albert Einstein suggested in his statement above, either you decide to believe the Universe is for you or against you. Which do you believe?

Before you answer the question, you might want to consider this perspective from quantum physics: The world we live in is neither inert nor passive. It is alive, awake, and aware; and energetically responsive to our thoughts. Yes, everyone's thoughts.

New Thought leader, writer, and teacher, Ernest Holmes, explained it in this way: "There is a Power around you that knows and understands all things. Its presence permeates everything, binding all together in one complete whole. This Power works like the soil; it receives the seed of your thought and at once begins to operate upon it."

In other words, the Universe vibrates in sync with you, sending back the energy of the thoughts and experiences that you initiate—sometimes immediately, sometimes much later. But always with the same flavor. Metaphysicians say that the moment we initiate a thought or action, the result is initiated as well and will return to us like a boomerang, unless we interrupt the return by an intentional mitigating action.

"Trust your soul because your soul not only trusts the good in life, it is a part of the good."

While it may seem daunting to imagine that the Universe is somehow keeping score, it is also reassuring that there is order in the Universe and that our own thoughts and actions result in corresponding energetic feedback experiences. You are not at the mercy of a controlling Universe; you are co-creating your reality with it.

This fact can be exciting. If you think of the Universe as benevolent, it means you believe it is caring, helpful, compassionate, magnanimous—bringing good things your way. You realize that you are always being supported and that you are loved and looked after no matter what is happening in your life. You are never alone. You are part of a conscious whole.

Believing "life is for you" might be a big shift in perspective for you, but it is a shift that is worth making. It will change your life—in all the right ways—resulting in a reassuring knowing that all is well no matter how it appears. The Universe is conspiring for good in your favor.

As you recall in the Introduction, your soul essence is a part of a universal Spirit. As you align your personality with your soul, you align yourself with this benevolence. Trust your soul because your soul not only trusts the good in life, it is a part of the good. In fact, as you line up with benevolence, your soul emanates happiness through you. Your level of ease and contentment are evidence that you are in congruence with your soul and naturally receiving your good. You are congruent with a Divine Order, and you understand the power of the prayer, "Thy will and my will are one." Yes. Life is for you, and life is working through you, too. You are in a co-creative partnership with life.

My friend Karrie still remembers a night many years ago when she was returning from the airport, after having dropped off family members after the holidays. It was late, snowy, and dark; and she got sleepy. In fact, she dozed off at the wheel. Suddenly, she heard a voice inside her head proclaim loudly, "Wake up." She did and noticed she was only a few feet away from a slippery bridge that was covered in ice. She is certain that the wake-up call saved her life. One second more and she would have tumbled into a vast ravine.

"In a responsive and loving Universe, you get help when you need it, and you can also ask for help."

In a responsive and loving Universe, you get help when you need it, and you can also ask for help. A well-known verse in the *Bible* says: "Ask, and it will be given to you. Seek, and you will find. Knock, and the door will be opened to you." That advice turns out to be true. Your requests are being answered. When you trust in benevolence, you notice the blessings. When you look for good, you see it. When you need counsel, answers will arrive to you. You can experiment with this idea and enjoy the results.

On the other hand, if you think the Universe is threatening, punitive, or controlling, it will reflect those experiences back to you. If you create a story that life is out to get you, your experiences will be played out from that point of view again and again. You will live on the defensive.

I bet you know what I mean. You probably have a friend or family member who can only see what's wrong. She says things like, "I'm terrible with money. I just don't have the Midas touch." And then what happens? She buys when the market is high and sells when it is low. And she does this over and over again because she simply expects it to be that way. She's trained her mind to believe misfortune is her lot in life.

Maybe you know someone who experienced a couple of difficult romantic relationships and concludes, "I'm not lucky in love." What happens to him? He continues to be attracted to dating partners who hurt him, create drama, and leave him feeling lonely. He might even give up on love. Unconsciously, he looks for evidence (more bad relationships) to justify his faulty beliefs, when, in fact, the world is actually reflecting back his own negative thoughts.

Our attention is a powerful force: What we focus on grows; it's where the energy flows. So, if you focus on the good, you open your mind to receive the best that life has to give. When your mind is positively directed, you can find many blessings in your life. Once you begin looking for what's right, you will find it. Misdirected, your mind is likely to see many flaws in yourself and in your life.

So, what do you say? Are you ready to co-create your reality? Is the Universe friendly or hostile? This is the choice you can make.

Just so we are clear here: The view you choose to live by dictates your responses to what happens to you, and it attracts more of the same. A famous Zen story illustrates this point:

A traveler was visiting a village and wondered what it might be like to live there. He asked a Zen master he met on the road, 'Do you think I will like the people in this village?' The master replied with a question of his own: 'How are the people in the village where you come from?' 'They are wicked: Greedy cheats and liars.'

'Those are the same kind of people who live here,' replied the master.

Not long thereafter another traveler also asked the Zen master if the same village might be suitable for him to live in. Once again, the master asked, 'What kind of people live in your village?' 'They are wonderful and caring and look out for each other,' was the response. 'Those are the very same type of people who live here.'

Attributes of Wisdom One – Life Is for You:

- Trusting
- Optimistic
- Hopeful
- Confident
- Relaxed
- Allowing

Empowered to Change

The more we go down the rabbit hole of physics, the more we realize that we affect each other. We are "entangled." We influence each other no matter how far apart we are in space and time. So, one small action in one place can lead to a huge result elsewhere. (You have probably heard about this; it's called the Butterfly Effect.) If we have that kind of power to influence life, why would so many people choose limiting thoughts? Why would people doubt? Why would we expect anything other than good?

It's because our conditioned programs rule us. But that conditioning, what we were trained to believe, is flexible.

It is my hope that through this journey you will stretch beyond limiting programs into an empowered self. Yes, a soul inspired life means you are empowered, not a victim. This transformation takes diligence and determination to bring awareness to your fearful patterns and to change them. Bruce Lipton, author of *Biology of Belief*, teaches that ninety-five percent of our behavior is derived from programs, seventy percent of which are dysfunctional and downloaded before age seven by parents, siblings, and our community. Then, the subconscious mind, which automatically acts on this programming, takes control of our behavior and physiology.

I can confidently tell you, based on my own experience, that the foundation of a soul inspired life is to become aware of fear-based beliefs, challenge them, and choose more loving beliefs. The first of the Seven Wisdoms calls you to hold steady in the belief of a friendly Universe. If you are not there yet, don't worry. The lens from which you view life can change as easily as putting on a pair of rose-colored glasses. Suddenly, life will look very different, and how it looked before will be but a memory. Be prepared, though, for the challenges that might accompany this paradigm shift when things are hard. A helpful approach is to suspend premature judgment.

Give everything time to unfold at its own pace, and you *will* count your blessings in time. Have you heard the *Reader's Digest* story about the farmer's wife who lost her wedding ring, and then found it one day when she cut into a baked potato?

In hindsight, you may see why something transpired and recognize it as a blessing—a part of your soul journey. Trust allows you to believe it now, before you have the evidence.

If you go back to the past and review your life with the lens of trust, you will begin to see more of the goodness that came from your experiences. What has happened to you? Who have you met? Where have you traveled or lived? What jobs have you had? From those experiences what were the blessings or assets you gained? Even if you resisted or got angry when things did not go your way (or go at your desired pace), can you now see that the Benevolent Universe was at play?

It is healing to review and find the gifts from your past. It is magical to trust right now that Life is For You.

Sometimes, it's obvious when good things come our way: We win a prize, we get the job, receive a bonus, find something we have lost, make a wonderful new friend, fall in love, or get upgraded to first class. That's us living with the green light on. The more we expect good, notice it, and appreciate it, the more good we seem to get. Under those conditions, it is easy to believe that "life is for me!" But sometimes the good is hidden in what can appear, at first sight, to be a catastrophe. Sometimes life needs to play out a little more to reveal the good, and our work is to be patient and expectant of the blessings to come.

This Too Is for the Good

My root spiritual teacher, David, instilled this understanding in me as he modeled trust and patience. He often shared the story of a rabbinic sage who was asked by his students, "What is the most important thing for us to believe?" The rabbi replied, "This too is for the good."

I experienced the profundity of this statement firsthand some years ago when my parents' home caught on fire. Flames destroyed most of their home and personal possessions, and my Dad faced a life-threatening heart attack and bypass surgery at the same time. Yes, in an instant and all at once, devastation hit our lives.

It was a beautiful Saturday morning in December. As I was packing up the car for what I thought would be an adventurous day of skiing, the phone rang. "Good morning," I said casually. Then I heard alarm in Mom's voice. "The house is on fire, and your Dad is not doing so well." Waves of shock ran through me.

Within fifteen minutes I was on the road with boxes and extra clothes. When I arrived on the scene two hours later, my Father had been rushed in an ambulance to the hospital, and my Mom stood across from the house in her robe, watching much of what she knew as home charred or turned to ashes.

Mom changed into the blue jeans and a sweater I had packed, and I drove her to the hospital to see Dad. We were told that he had suffered a minor heart attack and that he needed to be transferred to a hospital in a larger city for more tests.

This scenario sounds like it could be the worst thing that could have happened to my parents. Most people would be arguing with God, cursing, and venting anger—feeling victimized and sorry for themselves. Or blaming each other for the electrical fuse that went awry in the home sauna that caused the fire. But to my amazement, my parents chose not to blame but rather to see the good. From the very start, they responded with a willingness to find the blessings in the disaster.

I firmly believe that their resolve to take the high road was seeded in a philosophy that they had adopted many years prior. They knew that there are gifts in everything that happens. When Mom and Dad started looking for the blessings in their loss, they found them.

What were the gifts?

Blessing Number One: Because of the fire, my Dad was shocked into a heart attack, which triggered emergency medical tests that identified his need for a five-way bypass. Had there been no fire, he may have waited too long before recognizing his need for surgery. He may have had a bigger, even deadly, heart attack later.

Blessing Number Two: With the fire came life alterations: simplification, purification, and renovation. Some precious memorabilia and heirlooms were forever gone, but my parents' priorities had changed, and the memories they carried within became much more important than the material possessions they had lost. Their insurance coverage allowed an upgrade for the replacements they needed, and they let go of the rest.

Blessing Number Three: All the stresses that accompanied the fire and the painstaking recovery from heart surgery brought my parents closer together. They nurtured and cared for each other. When one of my parents was exhausted, the other helped out. They found renewed strength in their partnership and a more loving companionship than they had had before.

Years later, my parents still say the experience "was one of the best things that ever happened to us." The silver lining of their so-called disaster was their choice to find and focus on the good that came from it.

In the dualistic and fearful paradigm of life that is so prevalent in our culture, people are often too quick to judge and label unexpected events as being "good" or "bad." When friends share sad stories and dramas, it's easy—and even expected—to jump to conditioned responses such as, "I'm sorry. That's too bad. Oh, how awful!" While validating others' feelings can be a noble and loving first step, perhaps, after empathizing, we can do a greater service by asking: "What good is coming from this? Do you see a gift in this experience? How can you become a better person because of this?" These types of questions help people reframe their experiences and make empowered choices.

You always have the choice to meet life with disappointment or meet life with an open mind and expect something advantageous to come. Trust encourages you to do the latter. Some popular and well-documented inventions grew out of disasters or mistakes: from chocolate chip cookies and popsicles to inkjet printers, Post-its, and Velcro. All it took was embracing serendipity and a change in perspective, one that realizes, "Life is for me."

The movement of the Universe is complex in its benevolence, and it is useless to classify something that happens to us or others as right or wrong. The consequences of actions are playing out in a celestial accordance here on planet Earth. And while dualistic thinking is the norm on Earth, we have a choice to transcend black-and-white thinking. The following Taoist parable, one that my father taught us growing up, illustrates this very point. While the neighbors in the story judge through a dualistic view, the farmer maintains neutrality and faith.

> *A Chinese farmer gets a horse, which soon runs away. The neighbors commiserate and say, 'How unfortunate.' The farmer says, 'It could be good; it could be bad. Who knows?'*
>
> *The horse comes back and brings three other wild horses with him. The surprised neighbors say, 'What good fortune.' The farmer repeats, 'It could be good; it could be bad. Who knows?'*
>
> *The farmer's son decides to ride one of the wild horses, is thrown, and breaks his leg. The neighbors offer their sympathy. The farmer again reflects, 'It could be good; it could be bad. Who knows?'*
>
> *The following week, the Emperor's men come to the village to draft young men into the army. The farmer's son is spared because of his broken leg. 'How wonderful!' the neighbors exclaim. The farmer says, 'It could be good; it could be bad. Who knows?' . . .*

And so, life continues for the farmer of the fable and for you and me. Are you understanding the core message of Wisdom One? Nothing ought to be categorized as bad. Life is dancing with life for our benefit.

Some very successful people today once experienced "apparent" setbacks. Microsoft legend Bill Gates had a business prior to Microsoft, Traf-o-Data, which failed. Steven King, master of the horror story, was rejected thirty times before his first novel was published. You, too, have had "apparent" setbacks.

When setbacks occur, if you trust in the play of a Benevolent Universe, you will accept that there is more going on than meets the eye. You have faith that it will ultimately be for your good. There is great peace in this view, and it comes naturally when you align with your soul, the wisdom keeper within.

The Universe Bends Towards Justice

Seeing the good and believing in a Benevolent Universe does not mean you deny that great harm is being done in the world. We know that there are hate crimes, genocides, and war. In the face of such events, it's natural to feel upset, powerless, confused, and devastated, even fearful. But it's possible to also find faith and personal power. You always have a choice.

People in pain often act out their suffering on others. But the world itself, the composite of all life, is striving for wholeness and committed to justice. Theodore Parker, American transcendentalist and Unitarian minister, spoke to this point eloquently: "I do not pretend to understand the moral Universe, the arc is a long one; my eye reaches but little ways. I cannot calculate the curve and complete the figure by the experience of sight; I can divine it by conscience. But from what I see I am sure it bends towards justice."

You can trust that bigger-picture inequalities are being worked out. Deep lessons are being learned. Long-term consequences of previous actions are being worked through. What we sow, we reap. What goes around, comes around. In the East, this is called karma, and it is welcomed when you are committed to spiritual growth.

Both the hurtful and helpful acts that we dish out come back to us, eventually. And not necessarily as directly as you might imagine. The players may change, but the energy is congruent. If you betray someone, you may later be betrayed. If you judge someone's character, you may later manifest that very attribute you judged. If you offer a stranger a helping hand, you'll receive support at some point, too—perhaps when least expected, but most needed.

While the Universe is quite accurately playing out the law of action and reaction on your behalf, you have the opportunity to take responsibility for yourself—what you think, feel, and do in the world—and even change the circumstances with positive intent.

Viktor E. Frankl, a Holocaust survivor and author of *Man's Search for Meaning,* offers this helpful advice: "Everything can be taken from a man but one thing . . . to choose one's attitude in any given set of circumstances, to choose one's own way. . . to change ourselves. . ."

Have you been transformed by the traumas in your own world? I know I have. Unexpected disruptions, a broken heart, financial downturns, health challenges, confrontational foes, and petty tyrants have all *blessed* my life with life lessons that took me down and brought me back up again. Over time, I saw that many of the radical changes were indeed important course corrections of my character, not detours or delays after all.

When you look for the silver lining, you will find it. You could discover a greater strength, more resourcefulness, an impulse to contribute to a cause, a compassionate shift in your perspective—any number of qualities that could benefit you and others. It may be years later when the light bulb goes off and sheds light on the reason for a past experience.

While you can't make up for the hatred or hurtful deeds of others—that is something that they have to do for themselves—you can trust that the scales of justice will equalize misguided doings in time. It's not your job or mine to play judge. Leave that to the Universe.

What you can do is trust in your personal power and ability to contribute to a better world with acts of kindness, empathy, and sacred activism. This is truly the only place where you can make a significant change; and because we are all connected, as described in the theory of quantum entanglement, your change will affect the whole in some positive way. With Wisdom One, Life Is for You, you are not complacent; you are an instrument of life's benevolence, a conduit for awakening and positive change.

"You are not complacent; you are an instrument of life's benevolence, a conduit for awakening and positive change."

When you look around at some everyday heroes and heroines, you'll find early histories of abuse, abandonment, violence, or poverty. The deep yearning to experience something better inspired them to healing and giving back. Likewise, when communities are struck with disasters and devastation, like earthquakes, hurricanes, floods, and wildfires, people join forces to help each other.

Sebastian Junger in his book, *Tribe*, describes how people in communities undergoing massive threat or devastation pull together and call upon their inner strength to survive. They become stronger through connection and service to each other.

The Affirmations of Wisdom One — Life Is for You:

- Life is for me.
- Life is on my side.
- This too is for the good.
- This is a Benevolent Universe.
- I trust life.
- The Universe has my back.

If you choose to adopt a worldview of benevolence, you will begin to experience positive changes. Your status may not change, but your self-worth will. Your home may not be as big as you thought you'd like it, but the love that fills it will be bigger than you could have imagined. You may not have all the credentials you sought, but you will be credible in what you offer. This happens because life knows better than we do what will fulfill us when we have faith and trust! The external accolades and accomplishments come and go, but the internal feeling of well-being sustains you.

When one of my clients saw his business income fall by more than seventy-five percent in one year, he could have complained and fought the decline. But instead, he chose to find the gift in the situation. He decided to reframe his business and launched a passion project, a new consulting career with full vigor. The income loss was the nudge that got him motivated to reach a higher potential and follow a soul inspired vision.

Yes, life may be messy at times. You will experience loss. You will struggle. You will also experience grace and times of ease. Regardless, you will know that you are moving towards peace, growth, and inspiration, because you are supported by the most benevolent partner of all—*LIFE!*

With your resolve to see the good in all things, the good will be yours to experience. By remembering that "this too is for the good," you have the eyes to see the Benevolent Universe at play. By shining your soul through your personality, you realize you are a part of the good that is unfolding, too: You are the benevolent force moving through the world. Take that in.

More Trust and Less Fear

Nelson Mandela once said, "May your choices reflect your hopes, not your fears." In that statement, the South African anti-apartheid revolutionary and political leader recognized that fear leads us into making decisions that run counter to a paradigm of trust. Indeed, if we harbor fear, it has the potential to rule our life, leading us to make choices to protect ourselves against "a dangerous world." Thus, we lose ourselves in distractions, attachments, possessions, and other

mistaken ways of looking for love and happiness. When we live with a fear of lack, we are not able to be confident that we will receive all that we need. When we trust, we deeply relax and life lends a helping hand.

In my research, I met Emily, who aspires to live a soul inspired life. She marvels at the creative ways the Universe has helped her out when she has felt "in a pinch," especially financially. Here are some of the surprise gifts that reminded her to trust that life is for her. Getting an unexpected refund in the mail, receiving a surprise call from a friend wanting to sponsor her at a retreat, selling a book she found at a yard sale for many times the yard-sale price, acquiring money as part of a class-action suit she didn't even know she was a part of, and in one day finding every item on her grocery list surprisingly on sale.

If you relax your heart and mind, these types of gifts are available for you, too. Helen Keller, American author, political activist, and lecturer, who was the first deaf-blind person to earn a Bachelor of Arts Degree, stated, "When one door of happiness closes, another opens, but we often look so long at the closed door that we fail to see the one which has been opened for us."

We cannot fake trust, nor push it. Trust is felt fully when faith becomes more of a knowing. That powerful knowing kicks resistance and doubt out of our consciousness. Trust enters and lights up our world, incrementally.

In the transition from fear to trust, we feel both in varying degrees. This is natural. When the feeling of fear arises, it is a good time to gently remind yourself of the power of trust. Perhaps you can keep an inspiring quote or a story from this chapter in your wallet or on your bathroom mirror.

So the next time you are experiencing a tough day, you could ask, "What terrible thing could happen to me next?" OR ... you could ask, "What wonderful thing could happen to me now?" The question will influence your response, shift your mood, and fill your mind with possibility. That possibility thinking can get you out of a hard spot. "What wonderful event could happen to me now? What new solution is here, waiting for me to discover?"

"What wonderful event could happen now?"

Hope is the doorway to faith. So, if you are having difficulty believing and affirming that "life is for me," try to find at least a little hope. Consider that there may be a higher order of life directing you to what is best for you. In that "seeder" thought, you can find hope. If that feels like a stretch, find comfort in the Persian adage, "This too shall pass." And when the hard situation passes and your mood changes, then you can start finding the good in what transpired.

The key to the First Wisdom is to trust each moment, knowing it is moving you in the right direction for your betterment, your evolution. Don't wait for hindsight to discover the good. Believe it now. Faith will not only guide you and give you strength; it will also bend the universe in your favor. And, here is a wonderful bonus—making a faithful energetic shift will relieve you of a ton of fear! You wake up in a heightened state of consciousness and life gets easier. Grace kicks in because you invite it. Yes, Life Is for You.

The Flow State

Sometimes you may have a strong image of what you want to create. You can get stuck in your vision, hold on tight, and end up fighting life to get what you think you want, when there may be a more benevolent path awaiting you. At times, you need only let go of your preconceived direction, the perfect picture of your desired outcome. When you hang on to an idea even when things aren't falling into place, you can ask, "Does my image or goal still match the direction life seems to be taking me in?"

A gifted chiropractor, Dr. Eldredge, shared a parable during a talk on healing some time ago. It made a strong impression on me and has stayed with me ever since. I remember it often when I need to shift to a place of greater ease and go with the flow.

A man is rowing across a river, and the current begins to increase. He has designated a spot on the other side of the river where he wants to land. Determined to reach that spot, he struggles and fights the strong current, nearly capsizing in the battle. Eventually, he arrives, exhausted, where he had planned to land. What this man does not know is that a ways downstream, where the current was leading him, stood a beautiful woman, who could have become his loving wife.

When he finished the story, Dr. Eldredge asked the audience, "What could have happened had this man gone with the flow?"

Navigating the currents of life requires some practice. Trust is a form of surrender. You must let go of control to recognize when and how to follow the flow of the river of life that you ride. The parable is not to be interpreted as "always take the easy way." Sometimes, you know you are facing a challenge that is only there to strengthen you as you persevere on your determined route.

But, quite often, the path of least resistance is calling you for a reason. If the easeful way gets you to your vision, consider it. Usually, you can tell by a *feeling* that the effortless route contains gifts and surprises. It is as if the way lights up with warmth—you sense blue skies ahead, and you go forth with ease. It will feel like walking on the red carpet or stepping on to an escalator. You sense the "rightness" of a choice, and you feel carried along without struggle.

When you are centered in your heart, you know which way to go. And more often than not, the currents of life are a superb guide, better than any rigid plans. You'll learn more about trusting your guidance in Wisdom Three, when you experiment with reading symbols and deciphering life's messages.

Marci Shimoff, best-selling author of *Happy for No Reason*, writes, "For those of us locked in the 'I'm in charge' and 'I have to take control' approach to life, surrendering starts by simply inviting ourselves to believe that our Higher Power will respond to our needs and being open to the flow of grace when it comes. This gentle invitation is a great tool for letting go and trusting life to unfold—gracefully."

If you ride the current called *now*, you understand that a moment-to-moment ease mingles within the flow. Follow the course that radiates love and learn to sense the luminosity of inner sight that leads you towards the doors that open just for you. The more you allow this to happen, the more you will find that navigating choice points gets easier and easier with time.

You will learn through trial and error. As you study your thoughts, your body sense, and the consequences of your decisions, you'll begin to recognize that a higher order is involved. My grandma often said, "It's all in D.O." By this, she was referring to the Divine Order that protects and guides our lives. She was a master teacher of Wisdom One—Life Is for You. When she passed on, I shared this poem at her memorial:

A Tribute to My Grandma

*I see happy yellow butterflies
Ascending to the fragrant skies.*

*Rose petals fall,
From heaven to us all.*

*A gift, from one beloved being.
She is eternal. Life is abundant.
This is her meaning.*

*Like the flight of birds,
Her words
Speak of truth and good.*

*D.O., as in Divine Order,
she would say.
And this I know is her sacred journey's way.
Forever, and that includes today!*

Can an average person live in the flow of Divine Order? Yes, anyone can live in the flow—no matter who and where they are. However, because living in a *flow state* is not the norm in our society, you must choose it! To break from paddling against the current will take a conscious decision and deliberate, focused action.

Sometime ago, I was challenged to let go of a new home I thought I wanted. At first, I felt that particular home was the correct choice. But then, as much as I tried to complete the deal, it was not coming together. Things weren't falling into place. The struggle to liquidate assets for the down payment kept blocking the move. Unease in my stomach also signaled that something was off. And, most importantly, my beloved, Kirk, wasn't on board. That particular home began to feel incongruent with our hopes of combining our lives together.

I decided to let go of that home. I stopped struggling to make it happen and relaxed, knowing that the Universe would calibrate and offer new possibilities. With the choice to release my tight grip, I opened up to the unknown again. In the relinquishing, I saw Kirk and I happy together—moving forward with a harmonious vision and a shared dream. A better direction for us did come in time.

If you choose with good intent and an open heart, you will be graced. The more you feel, "I am charmed and safe," destiny will unfold in the best way possible. Believing that the Universe loves you and that life has your back, you recognize that grace is everywhere—not just in one particular "fantasy dream home." You know you can shift and move with ease. And you will. You feel the vibration of goodness coming your way. You connect with the general vibrations of your graced future, not as much with the details. Unlike traditional goal-setting, you follow the resonance of who you are becoming and what lies ahead. And it feels awesome by the way!

Do you see how trusting that "life is for you" allows you to open up for better outcomes and even miracles? You might not walk on water, but you will walk on the Earth—witnessing and taking part in everyday miracles—with your feet on the ground, your heart full of love, and your eyes seeing goodness everywhere and in everyone.

Welcome to Trust Life Is for You. This is the magic
ingredient to deeply relaxing and enjoying life in a Benevolent
Universe.

Gems for the Journey

- The First Wisdom is Life Is for You. The action is to see the good in everything. The more you see the good in your life, the more good comes your way.
- The first step in embracing the Seven Wisdoms of a soul inspired life is to trust that you live in a Benevolent Universe. No matter what situation you face, you can believe that life is for you, that life wants you to succeed.
- Sometimes you have a strong image of what you want to create. You can get stuck in your vision, hold tight, and end up fighting life to get what you think you want, when there may be a more welcoming path awaiting you. Learn when to let go.

Walking with the Wisdoms

- Start an Inspired journal or purchase *The Inspired Guidebook*. As you read through each Wisdom, ask how it pertains to your life and record your observations. Refer to the Appendix and glossary to better understand new terms and words used in *Inspired*.
- Create Sticky Notes or alerts on your calendar that say, "Life is for me. This is a Benevolent Universe!" These statements become anchors of belief and reminders to trust.
- Look back at your life and recall the times that challenges ended up being opportunities or when hard times turned out to be filled with blessings and gifts.

- Download the "Two-Minute Trust Activation" at: *www.ASoulInspiredLife.com/wisdoms*

Inner-Views for Journaling and Conversations

These are sentence stems that you are encouraged to complete and elaborate on. Take your time and see where your writing goes or how a conversation unfolds.

- I believe life is benevolent because . . .
- Growing up, I was taught that life is . . .
- To me, the statement, "Life is on my side," means . . .
- A rigid plan or vision that I need to let go of is . . .
- When I think of the pain and suffering in the world, I feel . . .
- If I adopted Wisdom One, what might change in my life is . . .
- A time in my life when I found a blessing in a hard situation was . . .

Pause and Remember:

- Life Is for You

Receive the Blessings

Seek and ye shall find,
That you are already
found.
Relax your heart, your mind,
Receive the blessings.

Ask and ye shall hear
The answers from
within.
Relax your heart, your mind
Receive the blessings.

Knock and ye shall see
The door is already
open.
Relax your heart, your mind
Receive the blessings.

Receive, receive the blessings.
Abundant gifts are everywhere.
Receive, receive the blessings
And choose to share.

WISDOM

2

You Deserve Love

"When you recover or discover something that nourishes your soul and brings joy, care enough about yourself to make room for it in your life."

– JEAN SHINODA BOLEN
Psychiatrist, Jungian Analyst, Author, Speaker

When you imagine all the love and goodness of the Benevolent Universe coming your way, in the form of abundant blessings, health, life lessons, and opportunities, it feels wonderful, doesn't it? But if you don't think you deserve it, you will not see it, nor will you receive it. You might reject it, sabotage it, or think it is for someone else. Have you ever said, "This is too good to be true?" Next time, catch yourself. The replacement statement might be, "This is so good, and it's true! I deserve it."

Do you believe you deserve the love coming to you? Most of us remain out of touch with a core truth—the truth that we are deeply lovable, not some of the time but all of the time. How could it be otherwise? If your soul is the expression of Spirit in the world, it is Divine as it is—not some of the time but all of the time. No part of the Divine is flawed. Your soul may be experiencing life in a different way than someone else's soul is experiencing it, but both ways are suitable paths. Even a painful past can't take away from your basic goodness and purity. Yes, you are soul, and more love is coming your way so that you can be all that you are meant to be.

To receive these gifts, you cannot give in to feelings of unworthiness, nor can you play the old mental tape of "I'm not enough." Instead, you believe, "I am enough." When your self-esteem is healthy, you come from a joyous place, and you uplift others. You are the one who lights up a room as you enter it, the one who gets unsolicited compliments, the one who everyone calls "inspiring." You are not trying to get or be any of this. You are simply authentic and real, and people around you feel your integrity and benefit from it.

When you receive love, you live with a lightness of being, joyously. You gain authentic self-worth through acceptance and personal-care practices. In this heart-centered and soul inspired place, you are not a victim of your past; you are victorious in the now. "The past has no power over the present moment," says Eckhart Tolle, spiritual teacher and author of *The Power of Now.*

Inner-Honoring

It is not your fault that you don't automatically love yourself, nor think that you deserve life's blessings. You've likely been trained to think that the gifts of life must be earned. On the contrary, the gifts of life are like manna from the sky—yours for the taking.

Without even knowing it, most of us make the mistake of judging ourselves as unlovable. As spiritual teacher and author Panache Desai sees it, "We have judged ourselves out of our magnificence." We see ourselves as worthy of love sometimes, and unworthy of love at other times. When we make mistakes, we label ourselves "bad," instead of simply seeing the choices we made as being misguided.

In this paradigm, we don't honor or celebrate ourselves nearly enough. How often have you bought yourself a bouquet of flowers? Or lit a candle before a meal when you ate alone, or danced in your home? And if you have, have you allowed yourself to thoroughly enjoy these inner-honoring activities?

In fact, we are usually more accustomed to punishing ourselves either consciously or unconsciously when we don't live up to the expectations of others or our expectations of ourselves. When this happens, we experience shame, blame, guilt, and victimhood, which create deep hurt and low self-esteem. The troubling part is that sometimes we don't even know that this shadow side takes us over. To ultimately be free of the counterproductive conditioning you've received, you must become aware of your thoughts. When you challenge your fearful thoughts, you will be able to co-create the life you want. This is the golden ticket to inspired living.

Attributes of Wisdom Two — You Deserve Love:

- Honoring
- Accepting
- Present
- Empowered
- Compassionate
- Loving

'Everyone Casts a Shadow'

"Everyone casts a shadow. Everyone has a relationship with the fearful unknown," says poet David Whyte. In Jungian psychology, "the shadow" refers to the unconscious aspects of our personalities. It is the so-called dark side because we do not see its ways. But even though it is hidden, the shadow has power over us; it causes us to act in ways that in retrospect we wish we hadn't. It is a great deceiver, manipulator, and exploiter when ignored. The dark parts will rule you unless you consciously bring them into the light. That is the way to undo the control they have over you and to heal whatever hurts they represent.

Many undesirable parts of our personality are hiding. Our addictions, our angry reactions, and our bigotries are all there in the shadow. Our childhood wounds, fears, and the false beliefs handed down through our lineage hang out in the dark recesses of our unconscious minds. These tendencies often expose themselves when we don't expect them. We hurt others or ourselves. But you can learn to notice the hidden enigmas of the shadow before they control you. The shadow is not to be feared, but understood. Bit by bit, it is to be brought to consciousness and challenged. This is how you refine your personality.

When you react out of habit, you can ask, "Is this action coming from fear or love?" With inner-honoring, you confront your conditioning with power and compassion and escort fear out of the way. You see the conditioning as outdated. You choose love instead of fear. You act from love, and you deserve love.

Believe You Are Worthy

As you learn that you deserve love, you embrace your total self and realize that you cannot fail at life because, as Wisdom One maintains, life has your back. Will you accept the benevolence of the Universe and say "Yes" to life's many gifts?

When you do, your daily choices reflect your broader willingness to receive. You choose personal care: You nourish your body, mind, and emotions. You rejoice in your personality's unique way of aligning with your soul and relating to the world, which is as individual as a fingerprint. With this understanding and authentic self-worth in place, you engage in positive self-talk. You encourage yourself, and you become your own best friend. You are willing to work through patterns that limit you. Self-compassion meets your deepest pains, including the shame most of us have come to live with.

In a soul inspired life, you believe you are worthy and you deserve respect from yourself, others, and from life. And you extend that loving view to others.

Affirmations of Wisdom Two – You Deserve Love:

- I deserve love.
- I love myself, as I am.
- When I care for myself, my caring for others grows.
- I am enough.
- As I bring loving awareness to all my emotions, I transform.
- I receive all the good coming my way.

"With a steadfast vow to act from kindness to yourself and others, your life transforms."

If you have a healthy respect for yourself, others treat you with more respect, too. The opposite is also true. Sarah Brassard, author of *Inside,* writes, "Speaking negatively about ourselves broadcasts a message to the world that we are not worthy of love, respect, and compassion. When we disrespect who we are, it makes sense that others would do the same. When we speak negatively about ourselves, it's as though we are trying to talk others out of loving us."

As you realize that you deserve love from yourself and others, you exude the attribute of inner-honoring. Inner-honoring involves moving in the direction of health, prosperity, harmony, and fulfillment in a spirit of love. With a steadfast vow to act from kindness to yourself and others, your life transforms. You develop peaceful thoughts, honest words, and caring deeds that nourish a kind of mastery of life. As Lucille Ball once said, "Love yourself first and everything else falls into line." When you bring inner-honoring to all of you—including your shadow—you will find peace with the choices you make in your life.

Ways to cultivate inner-honoring include:
- Share loving thoughts toward yourself and others.
- Become aware of your emotions.
- Ask yourself empowering questions that lead to positive answers.
- Stop self-criticism; instead, compliment yourself on your small triumphs and large victories.
- Look in the mirror and say, "I love you."
- Challenge fear and choose love.

Your Summons to Acceptance

Yes, this Wisdom is your summons to a world of total acceptance of your lovable self. However, when you answer that call, you may still find heavy barriers created by your feeling of lack, subconsciously cemented in place by your past. Why? Most of us grew up with criticism and blame, resulting in painful, difficult relationships with ourselves and others. In some way, all of us were abused, ridiculed, ignored, betrayed, or violated.

What did your parents, educators, friends, enemies, and religions teach you about love and respect?

In all too many cases, we were led into a false premise: We were told that we should be punished for our misdoings. We were trained into believing a lie—that we are sinful, bad, or perhaps even immoral. We adopted erroneous stories that we were not enough. This abuse from without, whether blatant or subtle, will often evolve into self-abuse. No wonder most of us have addictions or habits that keep us from expressing our radiance and feeling love.

Such hurtful impressions leave their mark, shaping how you think and act toward yourself for a lifetime, unless you become aware and choose a new way. I urge you to choose a soul inspired way—honoring and loving yourself. When you feel love, commit to love, and recognize that you deserve love, life's choices become based on love.

With Wisdom Two, you become deeply aware and deeply committed to knowing your true nature: that you are love and that you deserve love in your life—not in a superficial way where you only know this truth intellectually, but deeply, where you believe you deserve love in your life in every cell of your being. If you consider your body to be a temple, as many metaphysicians suggest, you regard it as sacred, as the abode of the infinite in the world. Practice inner-honoring until this view becomes a natural way to relate to yourself. In that state, you will find yourself asking, "What would love do in this situation?"

"What would love do in this situation?"

Foster Compassion

Truly, not many people have mastered the art of self-compassion and inner-honoring. How could you if your parents and society did not model it?

By internalizing what was modeled in our childhood, we treat ourselves as we were treated. We may raise an unrealistic bar for ourselves; and when we fail to meet that standard, as we inevitably will, we don't know how to foster compassion for ourselves. Then self-worth plummets.

Wrong thinking from the start gets you to over-identify with your blunders. You see failure as who you *are,* instead of *failing at an experience you are having.* You may forget that you are love learning to love, and sometimes you miss the mark. The word "sin" comes from a Hebrew word that means "miss the target." While we strive for perfection, we won't always get there. As Brené Brown, author of *The Gift of Imperfection,* states, "Imperfections are not inadequacies; they are reminders that we're all in this together."

Who has not betrayed trust, cheated, trespassed, stolen, or lied? Who has not made a mistake that cost money, took time, or elicited harm? Who has not failed? Even Jesus taught this message. When the Pharisees wanted to stone a woman caught in adultery, he said: "If any one of you is without sin, let him throw the first stone." Everyone slunk away.

A Willingness to Witness

When you bring your fear-based conditioning into consciousness and challenge it, instead of ignoring or resisting it, you find true freedom. As you clear out the clutter in your psyche, you are better suited to be an instrument of inspiration. Inner-honoring is not about reliving trauma and suffering; it is about becoming aware of past conditioning in order to transform. If you allow it, you will feel the bliss of healing: it is like a soak in warm mineral springs—calming and cleansing.

As you gently explore your inner landscape, you find what gets in the way of your personality aligning with your soul. You sense the interference. As you name that interference for what it is, you automatically separate yourself from the interference. You identify *to* it and no longer identify *as* it. Awareness is the first step. Awareness is power.

When you clear the interference, you connect more with your soul. When you connect with your soul, you clear out interference. It goes both ways. As this alchemy takes place, you refine your personality and you become a better instrument of inspiration.

One time I asked my teacher David about his role as a spiritual guide. He said, "It is simple. I help people cultivate a calmness inside, an environment of peace, and a willingness to witness themselves. Over time, with this new viewpoint—that of loving awareness—perception begins to change."

As he described it, his students start to perceive with less resistance and miracles happen . . .

Life unfolds more naturally, trust becomes heightened, and relationships improve. When you put inner exploration and self-acceptance as a primary focus, then loving action in the outer world becomes a natural byproduct of the peace and progress within. Transformation happens. You live from a soul inspired state, not from fear patterns.

As you learn the power of awareness, it is important to understand that there are no "wrong" emotions. It is what we do with emotions that counts. Projection and acting out onto others cause hurt and damage. Denial builds up stress. Emotions want to be felt, and they want to move—not be harbored inside. The word itself (emotion) suggests the action to take—motion. When you open to love, you allow yourself to be *moved* by music, art, and life experiences, especially those situations that elicit tears of laughter or sadness.

It takes courage to feel. Have the courage. Scan your body and become aware of what comes up inside; and when you do, the feeling moves, you become present with yourself, and you experience relief.

Projecting onto others is one unfortunate and painful way that disowned emotions can wreak havoc. Often our denied emotions go sideways. One example is taking out anger on a loved-one, or some other person, who seems to be an easy target (like road rage).

Instead of being controlled by the emotion, notice the anger before it gets displayed at the expense of another. If anger arises, you will sense it, like a flame rising. Stop and notice it. The person or situation that triggered the anger is likely to be a scapegoat. The tendency is to blame someone else, when they simply exposed the anger already inside of you. Whenever possible, go into a private place and pause. At the very least, take a time out and breathe deeply before you respond.

Resist the tendency to want to blame and lash out, using someone else as your target. Instead, consider a healthy method of diffusing the charge of anger, such as, journaling, yelling into a pillow, exercising, and so forth; or working with a skilled therapist or energy healer.

Denial of emotions can also take the form of chronically putting others down. Perhaps criticizing co-workers makes you feel better about yourself. But could it be repressed fear or shame that drives you to compare and come out ahead?

As Dr. Robert Masters explains in *Knowing Your Shadow*, what is needed for shadow work is a capacity for self-reflection: "To stand apart from that which is occurring to enough of a degree to see it clearly." It is wise to stay alert to what arises— question your thoughts and intentions and become aware of your emotions.

Sarah Brassard writes, "If the . . . moments of out-of-control rage and panic are storms, then the observer [within] exposes us to a view of the storm from above. I have found that the more I practice self-care, self-love, and meditation, the more I am able to identify when the unconscious, fearful ego is at play in my life instead of the expansive, soothing perspective of the observer."

This work—observing your whole self—is the most powerful and best way to find deep healing. The good news is that you don't do it alone. You accept and invite support from others. Who are your buddies, mentors, or partners in a healthy life? Find your supporters. One of mine is Kirk. He lets me know that I'm special whether or not I'm breaking out with a pimple or my jeans are too tight. It's good to have allies that support your inner-honoring. He also helps me to see when I'm in fear, and invites me to observe and choose love. Honest friendships help us with our blindspots.

Addictions Fall Away

Sometimes fear can appear as an addiction. My client Molly ate to appease her pain. She suffered, stuffed, and starved herself in an over-eating/under-eating, teeter-totter disaster. It was how she played out self-punishment. Self-punishment, the opposite of inner-honoring, brought her to despair. Molly harmed both her biochemical balance and emotional well-being.

When her emotional upsets and pain were too great, instead of reaching within her heart for a taste of compassion, Molly reached out into the world for sugary treats and crunchy carbs. Then to avoid excess weight gain, she fasted on water for days and hit the treadmill for hours of calorie-burning workouts.

This pattern continued because she did not know how to bring loving presence to her most painful feelings. It persisted because she did not know that she deserved love, and she did not understand how to find it within herself.

The suffering became so great that Molly knew she must do something or she could cause serious, long-term harm to her body. Some of us need extreme pain to wake up and begin searching for answers and more meaning in our lives. We become desperate—and highly motivated.

Molly was determined to get back into balance. Using the simple phrase, "How can I love myself right now?" she stuck Post-It™ notes all around her home, on cupboards, in the car—anywhere she stored or stashed food. These notes encouraged Molly to ask herself that very empowering question. Each time, she was prompted to find an answer that was other than eating.

Forgiveness and self-kindness crept into Molly's life over time as she learned that she deserved love, and could find it within. Through inner-honoring activities, she embraced all that seemed unlovable to be whole again.

Often the way she would love herself was by taking a nap, journaling, crying, calling a friend, reading a book, relaxing in a warm tub, or taking a walk. Sometimes it was punching a pillow.

As she explains it, "One of my most healing activities was to lie down and feel my physical or emotional suffering without resisting it." She would scan the feelings in her body without following their stories. This simple practice was similar to the "letting go process" used by Dr. David Hawkins. A respected authority in the fields of consciousness research and spirituality, he recommended letting go to cure negative energy and open a path to love.

Molly had learned, like we all do, that even if she detoured with self-sabotaging acts, she would still end up having to feel the pain she was avoiding. When she masked her pain temporarily with immediate gratification, with food, eventually the pain returned, accompanied by guilt. The consequences of avoiding her pain (such as physical ailments, lethargy, and depression) became more painful than simply feeling the pain. Molly discovered that feeling the pain while simultaneously feeling self-compassion had a more therapeutic effect.

While Molly found her way with emotional self-healing, she also reached out for coaching support. You may want to do the same if you suffer from an unhealthy dependence or addiction. Find a skilled coach, healer, or therapist. The more you show yourself that you love yourself, the more addictions fall away. Their hold releases; the habits let go of you.

A New Relationship with You

Although we are all grown up now and don't rely on our parents to take care of us, deep down we still have a little child inside. And often it is this wounded inner child that is ruling the roost. Only you can parent that child moving forward. You *can* create a new relationship with yourself, with your inner child—one where, no matter what, the adult you responds with compassion.

Can you, at whatever brilliant age you are, honor your growth, your mistakes, your quirks, and your past choices? Can you honor your journey? Can you choose unconditional acceptance of *yourself*? There is a little girl or little boy inside of you hungry for this type of love, and your adult self has the power to bestow it.

My client Sam took this idea to heart. He bought a soft, friendly-looking puppet to represent his inner child. Sam's goal was to protect and care for this hurt boy with all the love he could muster.

You see, growing up, Sam was offered little support and a lot of criticism. He had a father who began abusing him when he was five—both physically and emotionally. He lashed his anger out on Sam, calling him names. His mom stayed quiet. Sam took the abuse.

Sam's self-esteem suffered. Although he held the belief that he was unlovable, he did his best to make a life for himself. He worked his way through college and landed a mid-level management job. He moved in-and-out of relationships with women, all of whom took him for granted.

Sam did find some inner strength to see himself through the disappointments. But, as much as he tried to heal the pain inside, he just couldn't get past the idea that he was a nuisance, in the way, and simply "no good" as his father had suggested.

Using the puppet he bought gave Sam more clarity and distance from the pain. Whenever his self-berating got hostile, Sam defended the child and spoke up for him, exclaiming, "Stop it!"—something he was not able to do when he was little. Then he picked up the inner child doll and comforted him with words like these: "You are safe. I love you. You deserve your dreams. You are so lovable." The more Sam adored and reassured the inner child, the more he found authentic self-worth as an adult, too.

These types of role-playing activities are incredibly useful to exercise self-love, and they are often part of the tool kit that I use in workshops or private intensives.

Wash Away Judgment

We all have a past full of "could haves" or "should haves." Now is the time to forgive and release regret. Ana Holub, author of *Forgive and Be Free,* states, "Forgiveness leads to better health and more energy. Life becomes centered on what is happening NOW instead of being mired in what happened in the past. You learn from the past and move on to a better life."

Forgiveness brings about great transformation. Change happens within us, and these shifts affect other people, too. Heather Salmon, founder of Black Swan Temple says, "When we forgive, we release and recalibrate. We bring ourselves back into balance."

Redemption is indeed a beautiful gift you can give yourself. And when you do this for yourself, you can do this for others. By letting go of judgments about yourself, you become less judgmental of others. Our compassion for other human beings grows with our compassion for ourselves.

To develop a firm footing in Wisdom Two, here's the challenge: To love yourself on a good day is easy; to love yourself when you've made a bad move takes some diligence and a solid stance in inner-honoring. For example, I remember the dreadful day that I performed original songs at a mountain music festival—before I was actually ready to go big time. Although I had serious misgivings and inner warnings against performing that day, I did not back out. When my time came to go on stage, I sang warm-up songs for a gathering crowd, and I flopped. I felt ashamed. I had overestimated my abilities, but I forgave myself. I felt remorse, but I held myself in my own soft arms of acceptance.

When you know that you deserve love, you take time to make decisions and consider the long-term consequences of all your choices. You do this because you care about yourself. You gain patience and learn to appreciate each moment and each step of your individual journey of becoming. The discipline of inner-honoring is not self-denial, nor is it self-indulgence. The discipline of inner-honoring is to be a disciple of self-love. You see yourself as connected to a greater whole, as an instrument of goodness, here to radiate and serve—yes, as an inspiration. You naturally live in spirit.

Self-Renewal Attracts Inspiration

Self-care is a direct way of nurturing and loving yourself. With a healthy inner-and-outer glow, you get into that sweet spot of joy and allow inspiration to find you, to support you, and to sustain your state of grace. Self-renewal is like preventative medicine. It is an essential part of my daily and weekly scheduling, and I hope it is, or soon will be, yours too.

When you feel good, good can come to you and good will move through you. When you are happy, you make better decisions, do better work, and are more loving to those around you. When you are honoring yourself in everyday activities, it is easier to trust that good is coming your way.

I'm not the only one who recognizes how important personal care is to creative endeavors, business success, and healthy relationships. For example, Richard Branson, entrepreneur extraordinaire, states, "I have always made my health and wellness a priority. The simple fact is that if you don't take care of yourself, you won't be able to take care of business." So unplug yourself from doing and relax into being.

John Gray, thought leader and author of *Men Are from Mars, Women Are from Venus,* also addresses the importance of renewal time in his latest book, *Beyond Mars and Venus.* He advocates what he calls "You Time, We Time, and Me Time" to improve hormonal health and overall well-being, which increases relationship happiness, too.

Lauri McKean, founder of "Power of Yin," states on her website that she was a "Type-A, driven-to-change-the-world kind of person." She admits that this pattern not only created a legacy of impact but also of overwork, stress, and burnout. She writes, "It took a toll on my health, well-being, and relationships. In fact, there were times when I felt miserable and hopelessly stuck." Lauri's gone on to transform overwhelming patterns for herself and others with innovative ways to infuse Yin characteristics of softness, yielding, and grounding into work and professional development.

So how can you renew and ensure balance in your life so that you move from exhaustion to enthusiasm? How do you create more sustainable energy for the long term? In self-renewal workshops and online courses, I encourage people to make lists of their favorite inner-honoring activities.

I know that most of us don't have tons of free time to take care of ourselves. I also know that at times we must address our body's needs, while at other times our emotions are longing for a release. Or we might be mentally off center and need to shift our thinking. Or we might be feeling spiritually dulled by our circumstances and are longing to be in touch with more Divine grace. So, let's explore the ways you can renew yourself—mentally, emotionally, physically, and spiritually.

Inner-Honoring Activities fit into three different time segments:
1. Two-Minute Resets
2. Twenty-Minute Turnarounds
3. Two-Hour Renewals

Let's start with Two-Minute Resets, which are extremely useful when you are ultra-busy and only have a moment to get refreshed. In the Appendix and *The Inspired Guidebook,* you'll find an extensive list of inner-honoring activities.

Some examples of Two-Minute Resets are:
- Drinking water or another healthy beverage (hydrate)
- Stretching out any kinks in your body
- Listening to a song with positive lyrics
- Taking a refreshing walk around the block
- Reading an inspirational passage from an uplifting book

After looking at the above list (and the Appendix), consider what activities fill you up and last about two minutes. Create your own list of two-minute activities that will boost your energy.

My recommendation is that you engage in one Two-Minute Reset every hour. Yes, every waking hour. Brendon Burchard, the founder of the "High Performance Academy," makes resets his daily practice. He sets an alert on his phone to remind him to get up and "generate energy." He says, "A power plant does not use energy; it generates it." We can be power plants too if we can generate energy at regular intervals.

When it's time for a Two-Minute Reset, your pick will depend on what you have been previously doing. If you've been sitting and thinking, you may want to get up and move. If you've been physically active, you may want to slow down and breathe. You'll know what to do. This practice is a discipline that pays off in high dividends, like pure pleasure and sustained energy.

The second set of self-care activities fits into what I call Twenty-Minute Turnarounds. These are the activities that take more time and space but result in a greater recharge.

Some examples of Twenty-Minute Turnarounds include:
- Engaging in a recreational activity or exercise
- Writing in your journal
- Envisioning your future with creative visualization
- Pursuing a favorite hobby
- Re-centering your thinking; assessing your negative thoughts and turning them into positive perspectives (See the Appendix where I explain "Start Where You Are Affirmations")

Now it's your turn. Design your list of Twenty-Minute Turnarounds and include any of my suggestions that resonate with you. Get creative with this list. These personal demonstrations of love are for your contentment. I invite you to enjoy at least one turnaround a day, and the best way to ensure you do this is to schedule your turnarounds as non-negotiable appointments with yourself. Commit to a conscious date with you, a date to honor yourself and renew. What are you waiting for? Go ahead; put it in your digital calendar or daily planner.

Next, I would like to introduce you to something quite delightful, Two-Hour Renewals. The brave and bold find time every week for these Two-Hour Renewals. Can you find two hours every week or, at the minimum, every other week to treat yourself to a renewal? Renewals foster big shifts. Two-Hour Renewals have the power to restore you deeply from the inside out. When you respect these renewals as special times, you transform over time. Truly, the renewals prevent burnout and overwhelm.

Here are some examples of Two-Hour Renewals:
- Enjoying an extended recreational activity like hiking, biking, or fishing
- Receiving a long massage or bodywork session
- Creating and/or reviewing your values or intentions
- Attending a personal development class
- Having a personal spa day; at a spa or at home where you do your own mani/pedi, plus a facial scrub and a tub (By the way guys—you would like this, too.)

You will want to find your own ways of deeply relaxing and feeling rejuvenated. You can create and store your unique inner-honoring activities on 3 x 5 cards, in your computer, in the Notes section of your phone, or in *The Inspired Guidebook*. Have the lists readily available so that every hour, every day, and every week you engage in your Resets, Turnarounds, and Renewals.

This will become automatic over time. You may like to develop standard routines or choose to alternate the activities. You'll add to the lists and find out what works best for you. The important thing is to schedule the activities in your calendar. Make this real for you! These inner-honoring activities are a concrete way to honor yourself and create a more sustainable and inspired life.

Welcome to Inner-Honoring   You Deserve Love.

Love yourself deeply and unconditionally. When you nurture yourself, you are able to nurture others.

Gems for the Journey

- The Second Wisdom is You Deserve Love. The action is self-compassion. Imagine goodness coming your way, in the form of abundant blessings, health, lessons, and opportunities. If you don't think you deserve it, you will not see it, nor will you receive it. You might reject it, sabotage it, or think it is for someone else.
- You are deeply lovable, not some of the time, but all of the time. It is not your fault that you think otherwise. You've been trained to judge yourself. You have the power to shift that training towards self-acceptance.
- The work of observing your whole self, especially your shadow, is the most powerful and best way to find deep healing. Awareness is the most important step in this transformation. Awareness without resistance or defensiveness will lead you to challenge fear and choose love.

Walking with the Wisdoms

- Catch yourself when times are joyous, and say, "Thank you. I deserve this."
- Learn and practice emotional-healing exercises such as body scanning, inner-child work, or emotional awareness. Bring a loving presence and observer mindset to them in order to heal.

- Create Post-it® notes and stick them around your home that say, "How can I show myself I love myself right now?" Put them in places that will keep you on track with inner-honoring. Act on the answers that come to you.
- Download the "Two-Minute Inner-Honoring Activation" at: *www.ASoulInspiredLife.com/wisdoms*

Inner-Views for Journaling and Conversations

These are sentence stems that you are encouraged to complete and elaborate on. Take your time and see where your writing goes or how a conversation unfolds.

- Growing up, what I learned about love was . . .
- I wish to grow in the attribute of inner-honoring by . . .
- A way I keep hurting myself is . . .
- I deserve love. I know this is true because . . .
- Something I disown about myself is . . .
- A time I really learned to love myself was . . .
- I experience inner-honoring and self-love when . . .

Pause and Remember:

- Life Is for You
- You Deserve Love

Inviting Night

The sun sets with violet and rosy skies.
A breeze blows mild, fresh, ocean air.

The vegetable garden rests, the birds nest,
and the young woman writes
by candlelight
in her cabin home.

On the Hawaiian Island of the heart center,
energy reveals all of itself to itself,
and the young woman writes
by candlelight
all of herself to herself.

The needs, the desires, the emptiness and denials,
The peace, the freedom, the wholeness, and shadows,
Nothing can be left out,
and everything deserves the embrace
that a violet and rosy sunset offers.

The fresh air and stillness
inspire total accepting,
and the young woman
writes by candlelight
in peace and
presence.

The more she looks to her fears and longings,
the quieter the mind,
the softer the spirit.

Fears and longing seem to lose power over
her when named and noticed and revealed.

An owl 'who-whoos' as twilight dims to dark.

The open doors and windows
invite night into candlelight,
and the heart of the young woman
writing by candlelight.

WISDOM

3

Life Is Guiding You

"The word 'coincidence' does not describe luck or mistakes. It describes that which fits together perfectly."

—DR. WAYNE DYER
American Philosopher and Self-help Author and Speaker

If you have come to embrace and internalize the first two Wisdoms, Wisdom Three will come quite naturally to you. Wisdom Three arrives to a quiet mind, and the mind quiets when you let go of the interference between your soul and personality, especially fear. Fear of bad things happening to you can keep you from expressing your light, and this concern has been mitigated in Wisdom One: Life Is for You. The belief that you are not worthy of receiving life's gifts was debunked in Wisdom Two: You Deserve Love. Now as erroneous fear-based self-talk pops up, you can know that the thoughts are not true, challenge them, tame them, or release them, and breathe a sigh of relief.

You are now ready to take part in a consistent conversation with life. The friendly Universe constantly delivers messages to make it easier for you to receive the blessings that you expect and are ready to receive. Take it in! In Wisdom Three you will learn how to access and understand the inner-and-outer guidance available to you.

Life is friendly, and it is going to show you how to get the gifts you deserve: how to receive your Divine birthright, how to succeed at your endeavors, how to expand your horizons, and how to revel in your relationships. Genuine guidance or insight arrives without effort, and it points you in the right direction. You start feeling and seeing the signs and symbols to guide you because you are in a positive state of receptivity and faith. You are more poised to see the good and see through what is fear and false.

Believe in benevolence, and benevolence will be what you see. Start seeing life through these optimistic, intuitive lenses, and life becomes the greatest conversationalist you've ever met. As your clarity increases, your insight and subtle perceptions will grow. You will start talking to life, and it will talk back to you, through your intuitive heart or through others.

Life's messages will arrive as insights and symbols. They may come through another person, a body sensation, a song, a random comment you hear, a prophetic dream, or any multitude of unique messengers. Don't get too caught up in the messenger—but do listen and act on the messages if they resonate with your inner knowing.

"Genuine guidance or insight arrives without effort, and it points you in the right direction."

Some years back, when I sat with Byron Katie, founder of "The Work," she explained that little "knowings" constantly guide her and that she acts on those promptings. One time she got the simple prompt to take her earrings off. So she removed them. Later, when she got into her car, she smashed an ear against the door. She knew it could have been a bigger injury if she had her earrings on.

In *Happy for No Reason*, Marci Shimoff writes, "People living in [a] perpetual state of surrender and trust often report increased experiences of synchronicity in their lives: amazing coincidences, uncanny 'luck,' unexpected aid, and perfect timing . . . When you experience a lot of synchronicities, it's a sign that you are plugged in to Spirit."

This is how prompting can work for all of us. Don't second-guess the little nudges. And don't fret so much about your choices—just go with them. Yes, you can turn around if you need to or start over. If you flub up, fix it. If you are off course, course-correct. My friend Stella Orange, founder of "Writing Your Way Home," considers her whole life a series of "micro-experiments." Sometimes things work out. Sometimes they don't. This attitude takes a lot of pressure off doing "the right thing."

Attributes of Wisdom Three – Life Is Guiding You:

- Intuitive
- Insightful
- Spontaneous
- Discerning
- Guided
- Sensitive

Life is Guiding You with Signs

Through the years, I've relied on life's twists of fate and coincidences to reveal which way to go. These life events have helped me reach greater clarity. Life's promptings are rarely what we expect. Nor are they predictable, because a soul inspired life does not follow a straight line from point "a" to point "b." Life is a curvy road to navigate. Promptings are often random. And sometimes they are delivered in a delightfully unexpected way.

I keep an insight journal where I record experiences that remind me how synchronistic life can be. Here is a sampling of some of the events I've written down.

Insight Story One: When I wanted to sell my piano, I had a strong sense to call Aaron, a new friend. I did not know if he was musical; I just had a feeling he might connect me to the right buyer. I was hoping to get some money to buy a new cell phone. I called Aaron. Not only did he want the piano, but he also had a cell phone to sell—the kind I was hoping to buy. We made a deal.

Insight Story Two: In the first year of living in Mt. Shasta, I mentioned to a few friends that I wanted to experience a small plane ride to see, from up high, all the alpine lakes, peaks, and sacred beauty around me. The very next day, I received a phone call from a neighbor who invited me to join a private flight that was touring the area. No, my friends did not share my wish with him. It was an impromptu call on his part. "I just got the impression to invite you," he said.

Insight Story Three: When a dear friend needed to move, I told her I'd help out: "Let's drive in the areas that draw you and get a feel for the neighborhoods." Sandy and I took off on the adventure, following our feelings as we drove. We took back streets and looked for open spaces and parks. Within a half hour, we came across a cute area and saw a "For Rent" sign. Sandy made the call. The owners said they had put the sign out just minutes before, and she was the first to call. This oasis became Sandy's home for many years.

Insight Story Four: It was a hot summer day, and I had a pineapple popsicle on my mind. I had been studying signs and symbols and decided to play a game with life. "Okay, if I see a pineapple or a Hawaii license plate before I arrive at the store, I'll take it as a sign to get a popsicle." When I pulled up to the store, a car with a Hawaii license plate pulled out. That was one delicious game with life! How can you make life more of a delicious game every day?

Insight Story Five: One day I attended a program where the presenter proclaimed: "Take care of yourselves. You need to treat yourself more like your cell phone. If you are out of battery, charge yourself." Right then, I felt a sharp and momentary spark in my foot, like electricity! I knew that it was time to "recharge" myself. In this case, my body was the messenger.

Insight Story Six: Four women and I were lost in the Los Angeles area, trying to find our way to a conference. We kept driving in circles. Meanwhile, my playlist of more than 5,000 songs hummed in the background on shuffle mode (an unpredictable play order). Amongst the wrong turns, confusing merging lanes, one-way streets, and traffic, we eventually found the street that would lead us to where we wanted to go. At that instant, the next random song came up: "Headed in the

Right Direction" by India.Arie. Yes, really! I consider that an exclamation mark from the Universe.

Insight Story Seven: One night many years ago, as I was settling in for the evening, I made myself a soothing cup of tea. The tag on my teabag read, "Allow things to come to you." Just a few days earlier, my Chinese fortune cookie stated: "Affirm it. Visualize it. Believe it, and it will actualize itself." Both of these promptings urged me to consider a fundamental shift from going after things to simply letting life show up and pull me forward.

When such promptings happen in your life, it is best to take note and heed the advice. Many profound coincidences have brought me love, success, and better health. If you think about it, you, too, have had synchronistic experiences that demonstrate how you and the Universe are in sync, such as when you think of someone and they call, or when you have a sense that a change is coming your way, and it does. It can be as simple as wanting a new purple shirt, visualizing what it looks like, and the very next day seeing it unexpectedly pop up as an internet ad. Perhaps you have a premonition about world events, and they come true. Maybe you have a sense about the outcome of a work project, and you are spot on.

Stay alert because Spirit wants to assist you on your life journey. Don't doubt. Move forward with conviction. Rest assured that what you want, wants you. In *The Alchemist*, a world-renowned, allegorical novel about following your dreams, Paulo Coelho says it well: "And when you want something, all the Universe conspires in helping you to achieve it."

Ester Hicks, speaker and philosopher, is similarly encouraging. She states that as you open up to your dreams and desires, they reside in your "vortex of creation." People and circumstances are the "cooperative components" that show up to help you get to where you want to go and receive what you want.

Affirmations of Wisdom Three – Life Is Guiding You:

- Life prompts me.
- I am intuitive, and I trust my intuitive heart.
- I am guided.
- I listen, look, and sense the messages that direct my way.
- I am open to synchronicity.
- Signs and symbols show up to show me my next steps.

Promptings to Serve

In addition to sending you personal promptings for a better life, life might guide you to serve others in the most serendipitous ways, as the following story demonstrates.

My friend Abe is well-versed in listening to guidance and acting on it. As an intuitive healer, his life has become a continual practice of following guidance, day-by-day, client-by-client. One winter evening, he had a strong message to go to Cliff Lake. The thought made no sense at all. There was a snow storm outside, and he doubted the road would be clear enough to take him up the 4,000-foot elevation gain to reach that destination. Why would he leave his cozy house and take the trek? Abe didn't know why, but he knew he needed to heed the call.

As he drove his four-wheel car up the steep roads, snow flurries obscured his view. The road got slippery. Fortunately, he was a seasoned driver and his tires were new. As he approached the alpine lake, Abe saw a car on the side of the road, haphazardly trapped in a snow bank. Abe slowed down. A young man and woman came running up to him waving and calling out, "We're stranded and freezing. We have no food or blankets. We've been praying for help."

Abe knew he was the answer to their prayers, and he understood why the message, "Go to Cliff Lake," came to him. He invited the young couple into his car and brought them down to town and to a hotel. This is how guidance can work in our lives if we stay attentive and act on the promptings we receive. This is the way of soul inspired living.

When pursued correctly, little signs and nudges become the guidance that help you find the next steps on your journey. But you must be willing to listen to life's promptings with an open, peaceful heart—not clouded by worry, skepticism, or fear. Your energy and intentions will influence what comes your way. When you are centered in the present moment, you will be able to sense the best course of action and the benevolent synchronicities that abound.

Intuition Is a Knowing

While life's guidance refers to the messages coming to you, intuition is your ability to sense those messages and respond without the need for conscious reasoning. Intuition comes from the Latin word "*intueri*," which means to perceive directly. To be intuitive is to "tune in" to your inner knowing and to follow your hunches, feelings, premonitions, and instincts. According to my teacher David, "Intuition is the ability to know without thinking."

In a more recent conversation, David shared, "Intuition is your awareness of the larger you that expands ever increasingly in time and space. Part of you knows your future because part of you is there already. Intuition is a knowing from that larger perspective. Intuition is specific to you because we all have a unique path."

We all have intuition, but too often we don't access or trust it to navigate our lives. While signs and messages from the outside can often be obvious in nature, like a book falling off the shelf as if to say, "read me," sometimes intuited information from within is so subtle it can be difficult to notice it, and so we miss these subtle messages. There are ways to strengthen your intuition. First, let's look at how to "tune in" to intuition.

How we receive our inner knowing will vary from person-to-person. If you are clairvoyant, you *see* or envision. If you are clairaudient, you *hear* a message or a still, small voice. If you are clairsentient, you *sense* the emotions and feelings of people, animals, situations, or places around you. If you are claircognizant you have clear *knowing,* and frequently ideas suddenly pop into your head; your mind simply *knows* it.

How do you perceive intuitively? Although most people have one predominant way of knowing intuitively, your intuition may be a combination of two or more of these styles. Your language will offer hints about how you intuit. Do you sometimes say, "I could *see* that happening," which would indicate you are clairvoyant. If you say, "That *rings* true," or "That *sounds* right," you have clairaudient tendencies. Maybe you say, "I *feel* that's likely." If so, then you are clairsentient. The comment, "I just *know* it" or "I *knew* that would happen," likely reflects your claircognizant style.

Study yourself, and you'll find how you intuit. Whether in a journal, an electronic note, or *The Inspired Guidebook*, I highly encourage you to keep track of the ways in which you perceive intuition.

Take note on how intuition reveals a message. Maybe:
- You *see* a bright light around someone whom you meet, and they become a lifelong friend.

- You wake up to a *voice* inside your head telling you to get to work early. You do, and someone really needs your help.
- You *sense* something good is about to happen to a friend, and they call to tell you their awesome surprise news.
- Or You *know* deep down that a work project (that everyone else believes in) is going south, and it does.

Notice when you have an unexpected intuitive hit as a voice, vision, sense, or knowing. If the "hit" comes true, remember what that felt like. When you dedicate a journal to the intuition you receive, you get familiar with the guidance that comes your way. As you make notes, you are likely to recognize more of the guidance available to you. You expand beyond your five senses and become what Gary Zukav calls, "multi-sensory."

Cultivating Intuition

We are born with intuition as an internal tool to navigate our soul's journey. Believe you are intuitive because you are. Intuition is always available because your soul is in constant touch with universal energy. To open to intuition may take getting used to because it is beyond the reasoning methods we have been taught to use when making decisions.

The more you let go of the need to know intellectually, the more your intuition will be evident to you. The more you let go of controlling your future, the more inner-and-outer guidance shows you the way to move forward, step-by-step.

Receptivity to intuition can come from past experiences, personal expertise, or exposure to a subject. In situations of danger or in uncanny synchronicities of timing, we simply cannot ignore the inner prompting. But we must be willing to let our intuition override our mind and our pride. It helps to become familiar with intuition's ways.

If intuition is the soul's voice, as many Wisdom Warriors say, it seems reasonable to become still to hear it. You can tune in with meditation, yoga, conscious breathing, and other centering practices. Find a quiet space to be still. Being outdoors can be a relaxing way to drop the stresses you may be feeling and open up your intuitive radar.

Imagine a swimming pool with a message written on its bottom. Now, if there are a lot of ripples and splashes on the surface of the water, you won't be able to see the message. It takes still water to see the words. Similarly, when your mind is full of ripples of thoughts and your emotions are full of splashes of moods, you miss the messages—you simply cannot see past the chaos on the water's surface.

Meditation, and any other activities that deeply relax you, opens up intuitive knowing. Yes, many of the inner-honoring activities can awaken your inner guidance. When you are in a deeply relaxed state, you fall into a theta brain-wave frequency, which connects you with your intuition, your creativity, and your problem-solving abilities. Accessing altered states supports you in increasing your intuition.

As you enter altered states, you have the capacity to unite with knowledge *beyond* what you normally understand— what you think of as logical. These states are beyond what we generally call the brain; they represent our connection with a greater source of knowledge.

Most of us also sense intuition somatically. It could be through body tension or ease, an energetic vibration, or, quite literally, a visceral feeling in your stomach. Have you ever had a "gut feeling" about something? Did you listen to it and act on that prompting? What was the outcome? I know that when I have ignored my gut feelings, I usually have remorse about it. Now, I pay closer attention and trust.

When your gut feelings show up, they may be more intelligent than you think. The "gut brain" is the part of the nervous system that resides in our intestines, and it is often referred to as our second brain. While the primary task of all the gut neurons is digestion, these neurons also affect our moods, thoughts, and health. For example, the neurotransmitter, serotonin, which regulates happiness, is produced in the gut.

So, notice your hunches and see how accurate they are. Monitor your breathing and what it tells you. If your breathing gets shallow and you feel tight when you are making a decision, that could be your intuition telling you to stay clear of the situation. Another warning might be a sudden headache or stomachache. If you feel a sudden peace, however, that generally means you are aligned with your soul's purpose.

One of my clients was in a dysfunctional relationship. The day she decided to leave it, she felt an energetic flush throughout her body and a calming sense of well-being. The chaotic emotions she had been feeling left her all at once. She told me that at that moment she "just knew" she had made the right decision.

Body intelligence and somatic knowledge are emerging fields. As a society, we are learning to interpret our physical signals. For example, high blood pressure, an unusually warm body temperature, or a tight throat all communicate something to us if we listen. Perhaps the body is saying, "calm down, chill out, or speak your truth." If we call someone a "pain in the neck," it often indicates that we think that person is causing us stress and may signal the need for a change in the relationship. When your shoulders carry the "weight of the world," stop and consider delegating some of the load. The body does its best to communicate with you. When you make decisions, stay open to what you sense in your body. Your body will not lead you astray;

overthinking, however, can confuse the signals you are getting. So stop, breathe, and tune in.

Dreams are another way to develop insight when you interpret the symbols. Often dreams are premonitions, or they can reveal unconscious patterns that need to be transformed. They can also offer guidance. I once woke up at the end of a dream as my brother-in-law was counseling, "Laugh and cry twice about something before you roar." I took that as a message to pause before announcing big decisions, and to investigate potential consequences and feelings before launching new projects. While the dream happened more than twenty years ago, I still rely on the advice.

I'll also always remember the profound and timely dream I had where Wayne Dyer, one of my favorite self-development authors, taught me a game at a playground. We jumped across benches and proclaimed what we wanted to shift in our lives. He showed me how to mimic my body into a frozen position that represented an old pattern and then he asked me to make a "Change Statement" in which I proclaimed a new way of being! Once I spoke my "Change Statement," I was to move about and flow in an entirely new way!

Who knows how long the dream really lasted. It felt like an hour in dream time. I awoke with a grand insight into my connection with dance, movement, and speech as catalysts for transformation. I've been shaking old habits out of my body with more movement ever since.

The more you become aware of the insights you receive whether in dream time or waking time, the more you are likely to identify them in your life.

"Stop, breathe, and tune in."

What Blocks Intuition?

When my teacher David speaks about intuition, he cautions to be aware of fears and desires that block it. Fear and desire are "two sides of the same coin."

A fear or a desire of a certain outcome will:
- alter your perception (including your intuition)
- control your choices (skew your judgement)
- rule your life (often unconsciously)

To sharpen your intuition and make better choices, you can examine and become aware of your fears and desires. Once you are aware, you have two choices: let go of the fear or desire or fulfill the fear or desire.

David says, "The current constellations of fears and desires are what drives us in life." We try to avoid our fears and the pain. We pursue our desires for pleasure. What we need to do is assess and decide: "What do I want to manifest, and what must I release, lest it shows up by default through unconscious means?"

Here is how this plays out in the art of intuitive living. Perhaps you deeply desire a relationship, and you meet someone new. Will your yearning for connection and your fairytale stories delude the actual situation? Of course they will. You are likely to project your desires onto a potential partner. As a result, you are likely to ignore red flags. Your sight becomes delusional, and you might even surmise that he (or she) is "the one." You do this because you desperately want to find the perfect partner. And to top it off, hormones kick in to mask your intuition even more. Desire overrides your reasoning, unless you slow down, take your time, pay attention, and let more of the truth be revealed.

Here is another example of desire obstructing intuition. Perhaps you desire a new career. You have an image of a dream job or lifestyle as an entrepreneur. Your hopes and perfect pictures are clear. And then some shyster comes along selling a program that guarantees you will create your dream job. You buy in before investigating the deal and sign a contract on your feelings. But wait . . . it was not your gut, it was your desire. And it turns out the program you enrolled in was overpriced, and it underdelivered. Now, this does not mean there are no good programs out there for you. But the point is to take a little time, get grounded, and evaluate opportunities only when you are not heavily charged with desires.

Similarly, fears can also hook you into wrong choices and masquerade as intuition. Let's say that you want to write a book, but you are afraid you are not good enough. You remember a teacher telling you that you could not write. When you start to write an outline of the story, an emergency comes up. You don't get back to the outline. Instead of scheduling another time to work on the book, you say, "Maybe it's not meant to be." This is fear masquerading as an excuse. Later, you decide to enroll in an online creative writing course. Before you check out, the website crashes and doesn't take your credit card payment. You think: "It must be a sign. I'm not a writer after all." You give up. But that might not have been a sign. It could have been a computer problem, and it was your fear, not intuition, that stopped you from writing the book—a book that could have changed lives and given you great joy in the process.

Fears and desires can interfere with and influence your guidance, and they don't lead to your best choices or highest outcome. If you are not alert, you may allow their shadow vibrations to skew your interpretation of life's promptings. In fact, when you follow the suggestions of fears and desires they become stronger and create undesirable future results and disappointment.

See how tricky it can be to follow your intuition if you don't study your fears and desires. Remember the inner-honoring activities in Wisdom Two to help you release emotions to create a clear slate and still the waters, the ripples of your mind. With experimentation and practice, you can navigate your intuitive life with greater objectivity.

When you are blind to your path, those around you might see your best choices before you do. They don't have your fears and desires. Friends often give a wider perspective to support us. You may call upon their perspectives.

Alone, we might get stuck in fear or be terrified by desire: "What if I start a business and I go broke?" "What if I move, and I'm lonely?" "What if I quit my job and go back to school, and I don't like it?" "What if I ask him out, and he says, 'no'?"

If you are going to "what if" yourself, choose better potential futures. "What if he says, 'yes'?" "What if I love school?" "What if I get rich with my new business?" Then pause, and tune in.

Soul Inspired Choices

As I've already shared, your energy and intentions dictate results and outcomes. Choice points are significant (sometimes critical), moments when you are called to make a decision that might change the trajectory of your life. The future calibrates according to not only your decision, but also the intention behind it. Choice points are opportunities to make conscious decisions.

The more self-aware you become about what runs your life, the more you are able to align with your soul path, not your conditioning, nor your fears and desires.

The motives, from which we pursue anything, predict what we create and the energies that help us get there. If your intention is personality driven, where you yearn for self-gratifying results and are willing yourself to the finish line at any cost, you may eventually feel empty. The external reward doesn't feed your soul. It is a temporary high at best. On the other hand, if your intention is soul inspired—to pursue the highest potential of yourself and to serve others—you will feel supported, graced, and prompted on your journey.

Personality-Driven Motivations	Soul Inspired Intentions
receiving praise and status	serving a cause
getting approval	helping someone in need
hoarding money	utilizing innate talents
gaining power over others	nurturing a passion
seeking recognition or fame	experiencing joy
feeling secure and safe	connecting in the heart
proving significance	following guidance
basking in gratification	expressing your bright genius
wanting revenge	doing what is just

With each decision, you can stop and assess if you are driven by your personality (including the frightened parts), or inspired by your soul (which is pure love). The next time a difficult decision arises, pull out a sheet of paper and list all the possible choices; then honestly access your motives behind each choice. It is rare to be 100 percent soul inspired in your choices; you will likely land somewhere on the spectrum of both your personality motivations and your soul inspirations. That is to be expected. We are all on a gradual journey of becoming aware and refining our intentions over time. Do not judge yourself.

Do you see why it is wise to question your intentions before you act? Imagine a salesperson who is required to meet a quota. She may ask, "Why am I recommending this product? Is it for me or the client?" When the salesperson knows it is the best choice for the buyer, she can proceed in integrity. But if the product is not in the buyer's best interest, and she succumbs to the *fear* of getting fired or the *desire* for a bonus, ahead of doing what is right for the client, she can recognize the fear lures and catch herself before she gets hooked.

In the same way, you may let a fearful part of you talk you into a safe decision, like staying where you are, instead of pursuing a dream vocation; or sticking it out in a bad relationship, instead of taking a chance on finding a more loving and compatible mate.

Trusting You

Life is guiding you, and you are a part of life. Wisdom Three invites you to hone your inner knowing with discernment and sensitivity while conversing with the symbols that guide you. You may appreciate the perceptions of intuitive people, and at times you may have found their counsel useful. But ultimately, the choice that is in your best interest is the one that supports what you know to be yours to do. So, trust your soul self.

It is not always easy to make soul inspired decisions. One of my clients, Julie, shared an experience, from her younger years, when she overindulged in psychic readings, valuing the advice of others over her own common sense. When a crossroads in her career asked her to make a choice, instead of seeking advice from her inner guidance, or a business advisor, Julie jumped into "dial-a-psychic" mode.

One time, before entering into a significant business contract, she had to decide which partnership agreement to sign. She was swirling in the chaos of the differing opinions of the parties involved. She began to feel anxious and utterly confused. So Julie reached out to a psychic, whose advice she followed. While she had no doubt that the psychic had intuitive gifts, the psychic did not know the full situation. She was not aware of all the details, as Julie was. The psychic was not in her shoes. But

Julie trusted the advice over herself. Julie gave her power away and made a bad decision that cost her thousands of dollars and a lot of wasted time. The moral of the story: Only you know your soul's path. The key is to listen to your inner voice of intuition. If you take counsel from others, really tune into what resonates as "true" for you.

Intuition works in all arenas of life, and I believe it will become a hot topic in business and a part of education in the years to come. In my business courses, I introduce intuition as "the ultimate leverage in business." What company would not want to predict outcomes in order to save money or make a better impact? Imagine being able to hire the right employees, foresee trends, and avoid bad decisions—at least most of the time.

Vishen Lakhiani, The founder of "Mindvalley," a progressive online personal-development company, and author of *The Code of the Extraordinary Mind,* tells his story of intuition at work. In a recent email to his list, he described an experience of intuition in a sales job. Instead of calling every prospect on his list, like everyone else was doing and like he'd been advised, he decided to trust his intuitive impulses. As he described it, "I'd go into a relaxed, meditative level of mind, run my finger down the listings, and call the ones where I felt an impulse. The impulse often felt like guessing, but I heeded it. I realize this makes no logical sense. ...My closing rate started rising rapidly."

Let Life Guide You

My dear friend, Peter Mt. Shasta, lives his life completely by following inner-and-outer promptings. He doesn't think twice about doing so. I met him in 1999 because he was guided by an inner voice to go to the Mountain Song Natural Foods Store and look at the bulletin board. That's where he saw my flier that announced I was a new somatic practitioner in town. As he explains it, "The flier lit up."

Peter and I have become lifelong friends. I was honored to treat him with bodywork, and he became a meditation teacher for me. He also taught me a lot about following life's symbols to find direction in my life. Peter's life of insight brought him many blessings. You can read more about his mystical experiences in his books, *Adventures of a Western Mystic I* and *II*.

One time he got the message to go out for cheesecake. Even though he had sworn to stop eating so much sugar, the inner voice he heard was relentless in urging him to go to the café in town that had the best cheesecake. Peter, accustomed to following guidance, had the sense it was not just his sugar cravings talking to him, but something more benevolent, so he followed the cue.

Gazing over the dessert case, Peter met a European tourist. They started a conversation. Soon, Peter was invited to a table with sincere aspirants on a quest to learn from certain spiritual masters. Peter had many personal interactions with these same teachers and shared firsthand knowledge and stories. A servant to the call, Peter satisfied his mission, and the Europeans treated him to the cake, too.

Let life guide you. Yes, the friendly Universe is trying to get your attention in the only ways it can—through the world of people, incidents, images, sounds, and your feelings. Listen. Look. Notice.

The benefits of following Guidance include:
- Showing up at the right place at the right time.
- Being more efficient with less effort.
- Seeing the big picture and still taking care of details.
- Helping others with greater ease.
- Enjoying creativity and imagination.

- Gaining faith in yourself and in a Higher Order.
- Aligning with your purpose to manifest your dreams.
- Avoiding dangers and mistakes for yourself and others.

Albert Einstein is credited as saying, "Coincidence is God's way of remaining anonymous." Was it coincidence that when I rented a post office box in Mt. Shasta that a previous owner was someone I admired—the bestselling author of *The Seat of the Soul,* Gary Zukav? I chose to believe that my receiving his old mailbox was a confirmation of my dream to write books, and it encouraged me to start a manuscript and seek out a publisher.

In addition, the P.O. Box offered a second blessing. As Gary and his wife Linda maintain a practice of offering books to prisoners, their organization corresponds with inmates who write to them. However, the address listed on all the books is my P.O. Box. I forward letters each month to the organization, and they continue to counsel and inspire inmates. I love being a part of this cause.

As the soul inspired life builds momentum, you will see benevolent grace transform you and good things come your way. By tuning into your soul inspired path with surrender and a heart of service, you will naturally know what is next. You will feel it. You will want it. And it will want you. So let life prompt you.

Welcome to Guidance Life Is Guiding You. The friendly Universe wants to deliver messages to make it easier for you to receive the blessings that are yours for the taking.

Gems for the Journey

- The Third Wisdom is Life Is Guiding You. You make conscious choices based on soul inspired guidance. Learn to notice the messages so that you can receive the blessings that you expect and are ready to receive.
- See life through intuitive lenses, and life becomes the greatest conversationalist you've ever met. Look for signs from the generous Universe—the friendly Universe *that has your back.*
- You will understand life's messages through your intuition. Remember that intuition is the ability to know without thinking. Follow your hunches, feelings, premonitions, instincts, and the small voice inside.

Walking with the Wisdoms

- Practice the affirmation, "Life will prompt me." Notice the coincidences, serendipities, and signs. Messengers could be a body sensation, song, person, event, dream, and other promptings. Start an insight journal.
- Identify the way intuition expresses itself for you. Do you see, hear, sense, or know? Notice your vocabulary; it will offer a clue. Keep track of what happens when you trust your insights and intuition. The more you notice, the more you will see.
- Investigate your fears and desires when you are making decisions so they don't cloud or block your intuition.

Review the personality driven motivations vs. soul inspired intentions.

- Download the "Two-Minute Guidance Activation" at: *www.ASoulInspiredLife.com/wisdoms*

Inner-Views for Journaling and Conversations

These are sentence stems that you are encouraged to complete and elaborate on. Take your time and see where your writing goes or how a conversation unfolds.

- I wish to grow in guidance by . . .
- A story of life prompting me is . . .
- Intuition is . . .
- A time when I really listened to my intuition was . . .
- The desires that cloud my intuition are . . .
- The fears that become my blind spots are . . .
- My guidance is telling me to . . .

Pause and Remember:

- Life Is for You
- You Deserve Love
- Life Is Guiding You

Awaken as the Doer and the Doing

Life is like a poem.
We don't always understand
Why a phrase ends with a certain
word, Until the next line
De-lights us
In rhythm or rhyme.

Living here on Earth,
We play our personalities
Like instruments in an
orchestra.
When there is discord,
The Enlightened anticipate and participate in the resolve.

Lift your voice in the chorus of the 'One Song'
Composed and sung today.
But do not perceive yourself bellowing in solo.
Revel and rejoice in the harmonies around you,
For we are each but one part
Of multiple melodies so grand....
.... Just listen.

The poem and the poet are One.
Arise musicians, artists, creatives
All embodiments of Love!
You – Me – Humanity
Align your expressions with Truth.

Awaken as the Doer and the Doing divine themselves,
Like the painter and the painting see through the same eyes,
And the brush in hand obeys the High Heart.

WISDOM

4

Take Inspired Action

"We delight in the beauty of the butterfly, but rarely admit the changes it has gone through to achieve that beauty."

—MAYA ANGELOU
American Writer, Poet, Singer, and Civil Rights Activist

With Wisdom Three you learned how to notice life's little and big clues. Whether you are given a whisper in your ear or a lightning bolt of insight, you are now heeding the messages that direct you towards your best outcomes. Knowing *what* you are being asked to do is one thing. Acting on those suggestions requires a dose of courage—especially when you must risk the comfort of the known, which is most of the time. In the words of life strategist and author, Tony Robbins, "Life begins at the end of your comfort zone."

"Knowing *what* you are being asked to do is one thing. Acting on those suggestions requires a dose of courage— especially when you must risk the comfort of the known, which is most of the time."

When your personality is congruent with your soul, you naturally take soul-aligned action in your life. Are you ready to be unwavering and follow your intuition? If you dare to follow your visions and benevolent energetic pulls, you can manifest your potential through actions that are aligned with your guidance and your soul's purpose.

Yes, as you continue to decipher life's promptings and signs, you ready yourself to experiment with, and eventually master, the fine art of living a courageous and heart-centered life. As the poet David Whyte says, "Inside everyone is a great shout of joy waiting to be born." Do you hear your shout of joy? I venture to guess that you do. Let's flip the switch to "on" and respond to that shout with a hearty, "Yes! I'm ready to act with courage and to live a soul inspired life!"

When you commit to fully expressing your soul through who you are in the world, without holding back, conforming, or playing it safe, you are living an authentic, soul inspired life. As Gary Zukav writes, "When the energy of the soul is recognized, acknowledged, and valued, it begins to infuse the life of the personality."

My marketing mentor, Marisa Murgatroyd, is a prime example of a business woman who aligns her actions with her heart and instructs others on how to do the same. On her website (*LiveYourMessage.com*), she states, "It's common for people with incredible gifts to try to hide their gifts, and try to fit in. To try to be 'normal'. . . until one day, fitting in becomes impossible. That's why our tagline is 'Be the Superhero to Your Tribe.' We're here to give you the tools and strategies you need to focus your power, potential, and purpose into the right focused action, so you can build a business that expresses who you are . . . and change the world in the process."

While her web copy is crafted with an entrepreneurial client in mind, the message rings true for most of us. Don't you want to be a "superhero" to your family, friends, spouse, business collaborators, or community? Or at least a happy contributor to the lives of others?

You Were Born for This

Inspired action is you manifesting your purpose in movement and form. When you change your self-talk towards the positive, you change your world. Your special superpowers—your soul's gifts—might be lying dormant inside of you just yearning for the right conditions to sprout, to grow, and to flourish. What is calling you now? Is it time to change your profession? Align with a passion and use it to serve others? Love with more honesty? Replace an unhealthy habit with a healthy one? In what ways are you ready to act, move forward, and create?

By implementing the first three Wisdoms:
1. You establish yourself in the magnificent paradigm that life is for you.
2. You know you deserve love, and you receive life's blessings.
3. You trust your intuition and the guidance that comes your way.

Now, it is time to move forward. And moving forward is not always cozy or safe; it is edgy and also exhilarating. It demands bravery and grit. However, if you are aligned with your soul, confidently sensing your way, change becomes more natural. When you act from your passionate heart, and you do your uniquely ordained work in the world, you find yourself in a genuine state of actualization, accomplishment, and achievement. The bold, powerful you appears with vigor and makes things happen. As the French heroine and saint, Joan of Arc, said, "I'm not afraid. I was born for this."

When you do what you were born to do, you are not forcing yourself into a life that doesn't fit. There is, instead, a deep attraction and confidence towards the right way for you in each given moment.

Yes, it takes a dose of courage and a sprinkle of genuineness to express the full you, to live a soul inspired life. So, what do you choose to do? How can you create in accordance with your purpose? How do you act each and every day aligned with your values, your morals, your consciousness, your soul? You risk, and you do it knowing you are in resonance with your soul and the Benevolent Universe. When you are in alignment, your fears will pale in comparison to the exhilarating expression of the most authentic you living on purpose.

Attributes of Wisdom Four – Take Inspired Action:

- Courageous
- Daring
- Heart-centered
- Authentic
- Powerful
- Vulnerable

The Power of Inspired Action

You have a unique soul essence—your spiritual fingerprint. Your potential is already inside of you: Just as an acorn knows it will be an oak tree, your soul knows its potential, too. When you let go of *trying* so hard to "be and do," and instead allow yourself to naturally develop, you will sense who you are becoming. When you spin your wheels mimicking others or wondering who you are meant to be, you are wasting energy. So instead of asking, "Who should I become?" Ask, "How can I align myself with my soul's purpose?"

A wise gardener creates the right environment for growth. You can create the right inner conditions for your natural potential to grow, too. Through inner-honoring activities, your heart opens to love, and by working with the many exercises outlined in this book, you water your seed of potentiality with self-compassion. You consciously and courageously weed out distracting and detrimental thoughts. You eliminate fearful patterns. All of this conscious and caring attention to your inner-and-outer environment allows you to grow into the beautiful self that you are born to be.

Inspired action is an outpouring of the real you; it's actualizing your soul's expression. When I imagine a world of people engaged in inspired action, I see big-hearted people being true to themselves and others. I see vulnerability and authenticity. I see individuals bringing out their best selves and inviting others to do the same. I see people who are impeccable with their word—who embody harmony of thought, word, and deed.

Inspired action compels you to utilize your personality to serve your soul. Your personality does not hold the blueprint to your potential. Your soul does. Knowing this, you realize that inspired action evolves best when you refine your personality and strengthen your talents and best character traits. My teacher

David often counseled me to work on my personality and character. He believes that cultivating honesty, compassion, and patience allows us to improve our personalities, and thus allows the soul to express infinite love through our persona. He said, "Your expression is dependent on what you've been given as talents and skills, as well as what you've been taught. It is wise to examine what you've been taught. Release the beliefs that come from fear."

David suggests that we keep the teachings that serve our highest good and ditch the rest. This is the way to get rid of the interference between our soul and our personality, which include the disempowering programs learned in childhood.

Taming the Inner Critic

Your inner critic is one of those disempowering programs. It is a fallout from unconscious and confused parents, teachers, or other influential people in your life; and it gets in the way of you and your brilliance. The good news is that it is not you. Once you know this, you will not let the critic stop you from your soul's purpose and inspired actions. Your inner critic is the voice of the criticism you received in the past, which became internalized and lives on.

We all have an inner critic. The real question is, "Does it have you?" Your inner critic is that belligerent voice inside of you masquerading as you. The voice that impersonates you as you're thinking, saying things like, "I'm not smart enough. I'm not good enough. I'm not lovable," and so on. When you give your power to this negative voice by believing it, you feel like a victim and may allow yourself to be immobilized. The secret to overcoming the power of this voice is to relate to it as someone outside of you.

In working with clients, and in my own personal development, I have come to find that naming the inner critic is a powerful technique for creating distance from the harsh inner voice that can derail your efforts to take bold, inspired actions.

I call my inner critic "The Sergeant," and it shows up with a resounding, "No one wants to hear what you have to say." My response is clear, definite, and strong: "Stop, I'm not listening to you. You are not me."

What might you name your inner critic? Brené Brown calls hers "The Gremlins." Author Julia Cameron calls hers "Nigel." Other typical names are: "The Boss," "The Nag," "Lizard," "The General," "I.C.," and so on. When you name your inner critic, you exercise your authority over it and separate yourself from it. And while it tries to hinder you from your fullest expression by putting you down, you have the ability to stop it in its tracks and realign with your true self—the mature you who knows better, who has the fortitude and self-compassion to manage your mind and self-talk. You can say, "I am choosing right now, as my adult self, to not believe you. What you are saying is not me." Over time, as you get stronger, the voice of the critic will get smaller and less influential.

Robert Masters, in his audible, *Knowing Your Shadow*, leads listeners through exercises that bring this important personal work to life. Some of the sentence stems that Robert asks you to finish are: "My inner critic is . . . Her/his usual message to me is . . . I usually most readily believe my inner critic when... " By exploring your patterns with this negative voice, you can shift the relationship into one where you are in the position of power. You stand up to the critic with might and conviction and tell it what is true, right, and loving.

The next time you hear the inner critic, stop it as soon as possible. See it for what it is. Name it. Speak up to it. Say: "Stop. You are not me. That is not true." Eventually, the voice will retreat, providing you with the personal power to act in alignment with love, and to actualize your dreams.

Inspired Action Propels Your Purpose

When you consciously stretch beyond what is comfortable or familiar, and bring discernment to each endeavor, you flourish. If you cling to the familiar, you may feel safe and secure, but you lose the opportunity your soul craves. Explorers, pioneers, innovators, and adventurers know this to be true—life becomes exhilarating beyond what is familiar, safe, and predictable. You and I also know this to be true.

My friend Melanie Gow knows this to be true as well. Several years ago, she followed a prompting to walk the Camino de Santiago, some 500 miles across the Pyrenees, with her two teenage sons. All three of them returned from the 33-day pilgrimage changed. Melanie experienced catharsis and an integration of mind, body, and spirit. For her sons, it was a rite of passage into manhood. Melanie recalls that to follow the prompting took determination and "a certain amount of trust in myself." It also took faith and "the courage to walk out my front door and my comfort zone with no idea what the outcome would be." Courage is the small quiet challenge to ourselves to grow beyond our current limitations. It is our necessary companion on the path to true personal progress. Courage will bring you that horizon.

What I've noticed in more than twenty years of professional training and coaching is that new business owners and course participants are drawn to living an inspired life because they *know* they must stretch and become more than what they currently are. They know there is a seed of potential wanting to sprout. However, not all of them find the inner daring to do what it takes to reach new heights.

What's the difference between someone who will take risks and someone who won't? The answer is in the first Three Wisdoms: Those who trust life, who honor themselves, and who follow their guidance feel supported, and thus they become intrepid. The more you identify as your soul, the less you cling to your personality as your identity—your status or habitual thoughts. The more you understand your essence as a soul, the more heartfelt and courageous you will be.

At twenty-eight, I set forth in inspired action. I was led to Mount Shasta by inspiration's call. A bumper sticker I saw in busy city traffic advised me with the message, "follow your heart." That prophetic moment awoke a voice inside me that encouraged me to move. "I must find my true home." I knew I had outstayed my time in the city where I was living. Had I not listened to the prompting and acted on it, I would not have found the ideal life that was waiting for me. I left work, community, and all things familiar to follow a prophetic vision of living at the base of a mountain. I went on a quest to know myself and to create a new world. Miracles and signs led me. With my heart front and center, things worked out well for me. I found my sacred mountain home and lived there for twenty wondrous years.

When Jeanine Blackwell, a successful online coach and trainer, started her "Expert Called YOU" show, she first sent out an email to her subscriber list exposing her insecurities and the process it took her to get comfortable being uncomfortable.

The email began with, "I was the introverted, nose-in-a-book kid who had a reserved seat on the sidelines." After I read that line, I was hooked. "Tell me more," I thought, even though I had other "important emails" in my inbox.

Jeanine went on to explain, "It's not like I actually wanted to be invisible. I really wanted to chime in, jump in, be all in. But, somehow, the effort it required to put myself out there was so big that by the time I mustered up the courage to do it, the opportunity had long passed."

After missing out on enough promising work and life opportunities, Jeanine found that she had a decision to make—a decision all courageous creators must make—the choice to get comfortable being uncomfortable.

When we stay invisible and safe, we miss out on all sorts of blessings, like relationships, adventures, promotions, projects, and possibly even the purposeful work we are here on Earth to do.

Jeanine's process, like most of ours, required her to get out of her "not-showing-up" patterns in order to take inspired action. We all have choice points in our careers where we can sit back, be still, and wait, or we can take the bull by the horns and learn to ride it. When you stretch into your next iteration of yourself, you may start out a little shaky, but you will settle into your new stance in time!

Affirmations of Wisdom Four – Take Inspired Action:

- I am courageous.
- I act in alignment with my soul's purpose.
- There is strength in being vulnerable.
- I am brave, bold, and brilliant.
- I act on guidance.
- I create beauty in the world by being me.

As researcher and author, Brené Brown, explains, it's courageous to show up and be seen. In her book, *Daring*

Greatly, she talks about how exposed she felt when she decided to give her TED Talk in Houston. Today, that talk, "The Power of Vulnerability," is one of the most sought-after presentations on *TED.com*—with tens of millions of views. As Brown exemplifies, we can notice our fear and choose to act anyway.

The Courage to Act

When we are not acting in alignment with our soul essence, when we are not doing what we know is ours to do, we feel a general "ugh," which might show up as lethargy, apathy, or agony. It can be subtle or extreme. You might get sick, experience knots in your stomach, or live with fatigue. If you are not feeling well, physically and/or emotionally, this can be your soul sending the signal that you are out of alignment. What is your body telling you?

Unexpressed potential wreaks havoc on your body. Energy unexpressed eventually creates disease and discomfort. Holding on to your urgings without acting will clog your system. In Chinese medicine, this is called "stagnant chi," and acupuncturists identify the body's blocked meridians and treat them with the goal of moving the body's energy again, which in turn, impels us to act.

People who yield to apprehension's false warnings may numb themselves to avoid the upset that comes from an unexpressed life. Common numbing techniques include: busyness, overeating, drinking too much alcohol, gaming, social distractions, web browsing, or losing oneself in movies or fantasies.

Courage is called for when practicing Wisdom Four – Take Inspired Action. Courage will fuel your action and valiant behaviors. Courage is the power behind your voice of "yes" to your deepest callings and longings!

With a kinship with the first Three Wisdoms, you have become more certain of yourself and the positive outcomes awaiting you. You are guided into new situations, and you are prepared to move full force ahead even when you don't know exactly where you are going. You are ready to activate your potential.

With intention and focus, what was once outside of your comfort zone will soon be comfortable. What you thought unattainable will be within reach. And then when you are standing at the edge of a metaphoric cliff, and you know you are ready to fly, you will jump!

As you progress through the Wisdoms, you listen and learn from life's promptings and do not follow the interference between your personality and your soul. Instead, you clear the interference and unveil what holds you back from being a soul inspired human being. You undo, transform, and release any hidden or forbidden emotions, negative beliefs, limiting programming, or false fears that dominate your thinking and behavior.

When you are willing to look at yourself with loving, compassionate awareness and do the deep healing work of letting go, you clear the interference. Then, your soul-self can shine through you, and you bring a loving presence to all your interactions and experiences.

There are a few common interference tactics that hold people back from inspired action. These are the mistakes you can avoid. Look out for them in your own life and catch them before they take hold. Then you will joyously choose to act aligned with your soul.

- *Acting from unconscious patterns of approval.* People stoop to their need to please or their desire to fit in, and don't stand up for what is right. They find comfort in the familiar norms of society or care-taking.

- *Making decisions solely from the mind and denying intuitive feelings.* People push ahead on a project because it makes sense intellectually, but later find out that their gut feeling to abort or to wait was actually the right choice. This is a negative result of traditional courage. The bravery and bravado of action, or the "git'er-done" mentality, can push productivity ahead of its timing.

- *Clinging to a false belief that winning is the way to gain power.* When a person is after victory, the goal is the win—to become "king of the mountain," as opposed to the joy of playing the game. People who are entirely focused on the title, the first prize, or the top position, act without consulting their hearts. They want to conquer no matter what the cost, and they are not present to each moment as it arises. They are after external power and thus lose connection with their soul's message.

- *Refusing or hesitating to take risks because they do not fully trust that things will work out.* These people live in a state of fear. They are afraid of losing the predictable known, friends, a good reputation, money, security, and safety. They fear vulnerability and getting hurt. They hold back because of the fear of failure. They doubt and lose out. They forget that life is for them, working towards benevolent outcomes.

If you recognize these patterns before they rule you, you can challenge them. You can choose to live with faith and walk the path of a soul inspired life, even through the rough patches and blind curves—all the while maintaining flexibility to be able to pivot when needed or guided.

But you don't need to change everything all at once. That would be a drastic move and often detrimental. As you take action, take one step at a time. Yes, you can align your actions right now while keeping your day job. You don't have to make disruptive changes, you can simply add new activities to your life. Perhaps you renew relationships or make new ones, or study exciting topics. The invitation here is to follow through with simple acts each day that nurture your heart and soul.

Soul Inspired Relationships

Wisdom Four encourages you to act in alignment with your heart, especially in the area that means the most—your relationships.

Badges of courage are often awarded to people who have "risked it all" in the outer world—such as pulling off a dangerous feat, saving a child in a burning house, starting a business, or exploring the wilderness. But taking risks in your inner world, such as exposing your emotions, experiencing intimacy, and being vulnerable in love, may be the most profound risk of all.

It takes courage to tell someone you love them for the first time. It takes courage to confront a family member. And it takes courage to forgive yourself and others.

Vulnerability is inevitable when you are emotionally courageous because being emotionally connected to others exposes you to possible hurt and heartbreak. If you were conditioned to fear rejection, opening up and being vulnerable with others is even more daunting. It requires fortitude to face the fear of being left, and it takes conscious awareness to see the fear of rejection as a program.

Fears of vulnerability and loss lead people into safer realms, that of superficial and trivial interactions. This is how they protect themselves from the threat of being hurt. When people are frightened, they avoid closeness and spend most of their time talking about the weather, sports, the news, entertainment, or fashion. They constantly entertain themselves with activities like shopping, internet searching, social media, work, and movies. They become defensive. They put on a show. And they disguise their faults, insecurities, and difficulties in a myriad of facades and masks.

There is an alternative. You can become aware of the fearful aspects of you even while your loving observer challenges the fear of deeper relationships. You then create gratifying relationships and propel yourself forward in your evolution at the same time. The intrepid track is to show up as the real you with others. When you have doubts or questions about a relationship, inquire. If you need to share a hurt or apology, do so. If you are sad, find a shoulder to cry on. If you are afraid, someone can hold your hand and help you walk through the dark. If you need to take a stand with someone, do it.

Developing soul inspired, honest friendships lead to your spiritual growth. These friendships celebrate the intent to grow spiritually together. They are based in equality, and require two empowered, self-responsible people in order to be successful.

When you get honest and own your feelings, you learn to trust and be trusted. Friends, co-workers, and family members become allies. You are seen and understood but not judged.

When there are misunderstandings, amends and apologies flow easily, and relationships remain in integrity.

For example, let's say a friend turns down an invitation you extend. You could interpret the refusal personally and assume she doesn't like you and give in to your insecurities, but this might not be the truth. Maybe your friend is feeling overwhelmed at work or home, or she can't afford the activity.

A vulnerable act would be to ask: "Hey friend, when I invited you to the event and you said, 'no,' I felt like maybe you just didn't want to be friends. Is that true?" Your friend now has time to respond and explain that she is going through a tough time of depression. By questioning, you opened the door for dialogue and support.

In intimate relationships, aligned action and vulnerability are essential qualities. Honesty and radical acceptance create deep union. Past mistakes, white lies, and moments of remorse are best shared, not hidden. True transparency builds trust, and trust builds intimacy.

As you disclose your hurts and fears, you may recognize that the emotion is rooted in an unmet childhood need. When you share it in that context—not to feed it or even believe it, but to reveal it—you can say things like, "Honey, I felt hurt when you left the house without saying good-bye. My dad used to do that, and I never knew if he cared that I existed." This offers clues for your beloved to treat you differently, and it helps heal the wounds of your past. Next time your partner gets ready to leave the house, you might get a good-bye kiss!

We all have inner hurts, insecurities, and wounds. There is no reason to feel shame. When you realize this, you become defenseless and welcome others to know more of who you are. And as your friends understand you, if they love you and want connection, they will support your growth.

Are there really people with this kind of emotional awareness? Yes, you bet there are. Once you wake up and start acknowledging your inner feelings, you find others who are willing to feel, too. It's the law of attraction. To nudge these meetings along, you might join classes and workshops in personal development and join a like-minded community.

Once you get into the rhythm of being open in relationships,
- You share honestly and make deeper bonds.
- You get fearless and real.
- You stop pretending and defending.
- You stop hiding.
- You show up, as your authentic self.

Do you know what happens then? You start to feel loved, loving, and lovable. Becoming at ease with your own emotions, guides you to amazing relationships. You find people you can trust. You learn to shed pretense and be yourself. Being vulnerable is the foundation of honest friendship, genuine caring, and deep-lasting love.

As you are now undoubtedly surmising, the ability to act in alignment with your soul does not come merely from being vigorous, bold, and resolved. It comes from a place of love and support. Why? Because *caring* (whether it comes from you caring about others or from others caring about you), encourages *daring*. This is a biological fact. Oxytocin, the hormone released when we feel love, has been shown to increase our ability to take risks and can stop the freeze or flee (fear) response. It's not testosterone, cortisol, or adrenaline, as one might expect! No, courage is stimulated and sustained in compassionate relationships and in community.

To build courage, then, you do not need to be isolated and to "work up courage." Instead, you need to be with others who open your heart, which fills your well of fortitude.

"Being vulnerable is the foundation of honest friendship, genuine caring, and deep-lasting love."

Own Your Greatness

Creative energy is yours for the having. Hiding your brilliance is a form of shadow dancing that holds you back from joy. Mixed in with the shadow emotions, such as fear, grief, shame, and anger, we hide our greatness. All of us do it. We may evade our very own brightness by thinking, "Who am I to be so great?" Could it be your radiance and your power that you hide in the shadow and fear the most?

Are you hesitant to express a "big energy" and let your passion have free reign? Please don't let fear stop you. Someone needs your light to find their way, or some global problem needs your genius. When you think of it as giving away what was given to you, you see the service in your brightness.

Yes, it takes willingness to see your light and to share your light. When you don't own your brilliance, you project it onto others. You look out into the world and think that this or that person is the "smart one," "charismatic one," or "talented one." Do you play down your gifts or let others take on leadership roles when you are the more capable choice? Parents or educators may have trained you to hold back if they punished you when you drew attention to yourself.

Why else do people hold back their light? Some people do not want to appear arrogant. If that is you, give that one up. Here's the deal: Arrogance is just as egotistical as insecurity. Both attributes stem from self-absorption and are the result of being caught up in your personal identity and what people think of you. You can be great and unpretentious at the same time.

Other people hide their light because they can't believe they are actually that bright. This would be the case if no one ever encouraged you to share your smarts. The problem is that you are holding back on a lot of goodies that could benefit others. And worse yet, over time, if you deny the light side of your shadow (your brilliance), you become dull and uninspired. The challenge here is to have the audacity to own your greatness while being humble enough to see your greatness as a gift given to you to share with others.

Moving Past Your Fears

To take inspired action requires movement that propels you past your fears. As I recommended before, it is best to start with baby steps before learning to walk and run. We use training wheels on a bicycle for a time, and then we don't need them. It is the same with building confidence in any new area. Study and practice. Ready yourself for the inspired moments.

When Todd realized his dream was to be a professional chef, he studied the culinary arts. He experimented with spices and herbs, various cultural food traditions, and the specific processes and principles in food preparing that all fine chefs know. As he studied, he hosted fine-dining parties for friends. Eventually, he started his catering business with confidence and skill.

What fears are you trying to overcome? You can overcome the fear of public speaking by joining Toastmasters. You can overcome the fear of dating by asking someone out. You can overcome the fear of sharing your music by playing at an open mic. Sometimes the way to get over an anxiety is to pursue the dreaded activity and move through it. Other times, the way is to first study and learn before taking a big action. With other fears, you may choose to spend time with those who are confident in the skill you wish to acquire. Let their confidence rub off on you.

As you face the unknown and engage in new challenges, you may tremble, feel your knees shaking, and experience fast heart beats; but you can see all these symptoms as excitement, not fear. The bodily reactions of fear and excitement are similar. So, do not automatically label all the sweaty palms and shortness of breath as fear. Instead, say to yourself, "I'm excited. I'm doing this. I'm meant to do this. It's exhilarating, and here I go!"

You can also imagine that all that excited energy is fuel. The build-up is there to sustain the process you are about to take on. It is only uncomfortable when you are idle. Once you start moving with it, oh my! Watch out because there is some serious power behind your creative actions. It's like a racehorse waiting for the gates to open. The horse wants to run. And to live a soul inspired life, you want to run toward your passions, too.

When my friend Lucy Mazes decided to start a coaching practice to empower Latino women to be entrepreneurs, she had to overcome a lot of negative self-talk and the barriers that kept her from following through on her vision. She aimed higher than anyone in her family had dared before, and she faced the ridicule of her community. But this was part of putting her work out there in the world and letting go of the need for approval.

It took bravery to start her business. It took boldness to present her idea, promote her workshops, and do Facebook Lives. But Lucy pursued her ambitions: Her focus was on the women she could help, not on the opinions of others.

For me, speaking in front of large groups was "Yikes!"—a big stretch and a shock to my nervous system. The first time I spoke in front of more than 500 people, I was nervous. In the green room, I filled myself with positive energy: I jiggled in place and thought encouraging words. I listened to positive songs on my playlist. I pulled out all my best "overcoming-stage-fright tricks." This all helped, but the real key to overcoming the fear of speaking in front of that audience had nothing to do with those tactics or tricks. I lost the fear when I entered into a space of service.

When I asked myself, "Will they like me? What will they think of me?"—I became self-absorbed and anxious. The questions were all about protecting my image. But when I shifted over to asking, "How can I help them get what they need? How can I give them the best presentation?"—that is when the presentation became not in the slightest bit fearful.

As I shifted my focus completely to the audience, I knew that I was an instrument to help them receive what they wanted: inspiration! I entered the stage with enthusiasm and equally powerful music to engage the audience. I dropped my prop on the way to the stage but quickly picked it up, not missing a beat. Nothing got in the way of my giving everything I had to this room of salespeople.

I acclimated to the bright lights. I connected with the crowd. I spoke with them and found my stride into the flow of the topic. Everything I did was for the good of the group. The words that arose within me followed a well-planned outline, but the phrases were new and surprising, and the message was carried through my vocal cords with amazing force. It did not seem like me speaking. I felt the energy of my soul—something big inside of me—giving the talk. I believe that because I gave up approval-seeking, I was able to be an instrument of a higher good, and the presentation flowed.

Anyone about to do something great wants Providence to step in and do the heavy lifting. Rest assured, if you are about to do something profound, something constructive, something that will benefit others, you will have the assistance you need. Just ask for it, be receptive, and you'll get it. When you come from a spirit of service, fear lessens. You will accomplish great things in less time, if you put others first. The mission becomes paramount. As the mystical theologian and writer, Thomas Merton, once said, "Your life is shaped by the end you live for." If the end you live for is service, you are well on your way to inspired action.

Inspired action grows when you:
- Act from your soul purpose.
- Trust that there will be a positive outcome.
- Follow guidance and Divine timing.
- Care more about giving than what others think.
- Know that your self-worth is not dependent on others' opinions.
- Surround yourself with people who have accomplished what you desire.

Saying "Yes" to What Matters Most

If your calendar is full of obligations, how can you take inspired action when it comes knocking at your door? To make the space, you need to manage your "yeses." How? You employ scheduling techniques where core values dictate calendar commitments. You can also learn how to say "no" with poise, clarity, and respect.

When you commit to inspired action, you will be required to say "no" at times. You learn to say "no," with the bigger "yes" in mind.

I'll always remember how devastated Briana was when she had filled up her calendar with obligations and then was asked to lead a dream project. She couldn't do it. Crushed to miss this big break, she made a declaration to herself: "I will stop being a people pleaser, a 'yes person' to things that don't matter." She learned to set limits and schedule her time more wisely so that the next time she was offered an opportunity that she really wanted (whether work, relationship, or travel), she would have space for it. Briana had to learn the skills.

It doesn't come naturally for most of us to say "no." We make false assumptions that saying "no" hurts others. Well, that is not true—no matter what we've been told. Saying "no" is not rude nor impolite. In fact, if you struggle with pleasing others or overcommitting, you must learn to find peace in saying "no" as a service to all involved. Saying "no" allows others—the right people—to step in where you do not. Saying "no" builds trust in relationships. It shows others that you can take care of yourself and speak your truth. Saying "no" helps people know where you stand and what you want. Saying "no" helps you avoid regret, resentment, and overwhelm—and to follow through on what you say "yes" to. You want to "go for the wows" of life, right?

There is an art to saying "no" with poise, clarity, and respect. You can be kind and caring when you decline requests. In the Appendix you will find six useful techniques to make saying "no" easy and guilt-free. Check them out.

Jack Canfield, seminar leader and author of *The Success Principles,* says, "Success depends on getting good at saying no without feeling guilty." Seth Godin, author and former dot.com business executive, said: "Just saying 'yes' because you can't bear the short-term pain of saying 'no' is not going to help you do the work." Astrologer Tod Drescher, wrote, "Only take things on if they are truly what you want to do and are truly aligned with your current vibration. Learn to say 'No' to things that don't inspire you and don't fill you up."

Take Action Towards Your Dream

When you take inspired action, you move closer to living your deepest dreams. Deep down we all yearn for *something*.

The real question, instead of "What do I want to do or have?" is "Who do I want to be?"

Ask yourself, "What type of person do I want to be? What qualities do I want to exude?" You might answer: "I want to be caring," "I want to be peaceful," "I want to be funny," or "I want to be optimistic."

Now ask yourself, "How can I start being that person today? What are some specific actions I can take to be caring, funny, or optimistic?"

If your dream is to be more caring, you can start now. For example, you can clean up any garbage you see on the street. You can uplift the people at work by giving out sincere compliments. You can donate time with kids.

Anyone can do this. You can do this. Putting pressure on yourself to find a dream may be more futile than proactive. As your seed of potential grows in the right conditions, your purpose will find you when you let it. Opportunities will show up and encourage you to bigger heights. This all leads to a purposeful life where who you are becoming reigns over the outcome.

"As your seed of potential grows, your purpose will find you."

Taking inspired action is leading from love. No matter your profession or life circumstance, you can lead with love. You don't need to be a minister, coach, or counselor to be heart-centered. You can be a supervisor or administrator, a small business owner, a salesperson, trades person, an artist, or a crafter and lead with love. In whatever capacity is available to you now, and in all your relationships, if you come from a courageous loving heart, people will feel it, and your relationships will improve. Work outcomes will unfold with more ease. You will uplift those around you. You will feel happy and inspire others.

Welcome to Courage Take Inspired Action. Open your heart, express your highest potential, and courageously live on purpose.

Gems for the Journey

- The Fourth Wisdom is Take Inspired Action. Let your soul shine through you. Move out of your comfort zones and take risks. As you develop a kinship with the first Three Wisdoms, you become more certain of yourself and the choices you make.
- When you cling to the familiar, you may feel safe and secure, but you lose the opportunity for growth that your soul craves. Explorers, pioneers, innovators, and adventurers know this to be true. When you risk, you welcome new situations and become bold, powerful, and authentic.
- You can find strength and integrity by being vulnerable—with yourself and with others. Share your vulnerabilities with a friend, family member, or your beloved—someone you trust.

Walking with the Wisdoms

- Take a leap and do something out of your comfort zone. Make a list of some options, like going on a new adventure, asking someone on a date, pursuing a business or career idea. Experiment with ways to build your courage, such as listening to music; engaging in dance, exercise, or another form of movement; and speaking positive affirmations.
- Learn to say "no." Check out the scripts in the Appendix and practice them in real life. Take note of the profound

effects and sense of self-worth you develop by saying no with poise, compassion, and grace.

- Journal about inspired action. What do you want to be? Who do you want to be? What will you risk by pursuing a new direction? What will you gain? In which ways can you overcome doubt and take the next steps?
- Download the "Two-Minute Courage Activation" at: *www.ASoulInspiredLife.com/wisdoms*

Inner-Views for Journaling and Conversations

These are sentence stems that you are encouraged to complete and elaborate on. Take your time and see where your writing goes or how a conversation unfolds.

- Inspired action is . . .
- I am courageous because . . .
- My inner critic usually says to me . . .
- How I stand up to my inner critic is . . .
- My soul purpose is . . .
- For me to risk in the world, I would need . . .
- My heart is telling me to . . .

Pause and Remember:

- Life Is for You
- You Deserve Love
- Life Is Guiding You
- Take Inspired Action

Courage to Feel

Children laugh when they want to laugh,
Or tears come, and the crying starts
Then why's it so hard to express the streams of sadness inside?
When grief comes,
I try to hide.

Waking up, and I can feel again.
Waking up, and I can feel.
Having the courage to feel my pains . . . my joys
Living the strength to become,
I am the faith and I am
Living the strength to become whole.

Sometimes I think I've been hiding so long,
I can't even find myself.
The mind has lots of circles to keep me lost.
But the key, the map, the heart speaks,
Remember the child releasing in the moment.

What is healing if not feeling?
Emotion is a motion like a river flowing.
Move me out of this eddy of mind.
I want to be alive, like children,
or a river flowing.

Having the courage to feel my pains ...my joys,
Living the strength to become whole.

WISDOM

5

Learn as You Live

"Spiritual growth requires the development of inner knowing and inner authority. It requires the heart, not the intellect."

—GARY ZUKAV

Spiritual Teacher, Author, and Co-Founder of *Seat of the Soul Institute*

Once you have the heart and the strength to overcome your fears and take more risks, you will find learning on the other side of your actions. As we learn life's lessons, we evolve. Wisdom Five – Learn as You Live, follows action in a natural progression. As you express more fully in the world, you move forward, and you recognize the growth involved in living a soul inspired life. Whether you make mistakes or celebrate success, you learn. And as you learn, you align your personality more fully with your soul, and you evolve.

Learning life's lessons allow for your soul's evolution. It is the nature of your soul to expand in consciousness. Jiddu Krishnamurti, East Indian philosopher, speaker, and writer, stated, "The whole of life, from the moment you are born to the moment you die, is a process of learning."

As you recall, Wisdom One counsels, "Life Is for You," and Wisdom Five reminds you that one of life's greatest blessings is, in fact, your learning. You learn for the sake of evolving. Often, the silver lining of a difficult circumstance is the gift of growth. Your opportunity is to welcome your unique lessons and let them propel you to refine your character, expand in consciousness, and continually reach new heights of awareness.

In Wisdom Two, you were introduced to ways of releasing and letting go of old programming. As you *unlearn* habits and beliefs that limit you, you *learn* what liberates you. For example, you may have *unlearned* the erroneous belief, "I am unlovable." And you *learned*, and thus embodied, the belief, "I am lovable." Yes, evolving is the process of *unlearning*, too.

To embody your new learning is the key. As you integrate what you learn emotionally, physically, and spiritually, you become an expression of that new teaching. You show up in life and give tangible form to what you have learned. This is what makes you so inspiring to others.

There are no guarantees that your work, your relationships, or your creative pursuits will work out as you would want them to. Sometimes, we don't get what we expected or hoped for. We might be more successful than we imagined, or we might scrape our knees and *feel* like we failed. Welcome to life—a journey of learning. When you see life as an education and not a "test," you can open and relax into a more expansive perspective. You don't always get what you *think* you want, but you do get what your soul requires to grow. Life is not a test, it is a learning environment.

With the affirmation, "I am a student of life," remind yourself that you are not meant to be a master; but forever mastering. This means you don't have to be flawless. You don't have to be right. Whether things go as you hoped or not, you are learning and growing. Your evolution is the reward. Like a child curious about life, you explore your world with wonder and with less judgment or pretense.

Fun expands when you adopt a learner mindset. With an "open-to-grow" mindset, learning becomes more effective, too. You are humble and open to learning from all the experiences that come your way. The "need-to-know-it-all" mentality loses validity. Instead you think, "I don't care if I am right or wrong, a winner or loser. I am learning, and that is why I'm here."

Attributes of Wisdom Five – Learn as You Live:

- Learning
- Evolving
- Attentive
- Curious
- Open-minded
- Innovative

Approaching Life with Curiosity

As the namesake of the movie *Forrest Gump* famously said: "Life is like a box of chocolates; you never know what you are going to get." Yes, you might get some sweet times or bitter lemons. You might face inconvenient hard knocks. We all fall from cloud nine from time to time. We face conflict, scorn, disappointment, and loss. Although you may not have immediate control over the circumstances coming your way, you do have dominion over your response. And when your response is, "What can I learn from this?" you've taken the most important step to growth and spiritual unfoldment.

When you embrace the idea that you live in a Benevolent Universe, you trust that life is unfolding in the best way possible, for you and others. You welcome curiosity and discovery. This allows you to be inquisitive and experimental in your approach to life situations. And, you can be playful and amused along the way.

Being light-hearted is a side benefit of an inquisitive nature. When you really embody this Wisdom and understand that you are meant to develop a passion for learning, you constantly gain new understanding and your life feels spirited.

You will welcome new experiences. You will appreciate challenges and understand that feedback is constructive and in your best interest. Setbacks are opportunities, not detours. Stumbling blocks are stepping stones. This bouncing back from difficult life experiences is often referred to as resilience, and it is essential for growth. Michelle Kwan, a retired American figure skater, two-time Olympic medalist, and five-time World champion, shared, "The first thing my coach taught me was how to fall. I remember gazing up at her with a puzzled expression thinking, 'Shouldn't I be learning how to skate?' Looking back, I realize that my coach was very smart. She knew I was bound to fall many times throughout my career and that I'd need to learn how to handle it."

A good example of a person with a resilient brain and a learner's mindset is Thomas Edison. It took him thousands of tries to invent the light bulb. But he eventually succeeded because he believed it was possible. (Perhaps he knew that the Universe was on his side.) Edison considered all of his numerous unsuccessful attempts to be learning steps to reaching his goal.

There are other famous examples of entrepreneurial persistence in the face of disappointment.

Nick Woodmand, the founder and CEO of GoPro Inc., attempted and failed at two other internet companies before launching his passion project with the HERO camera. He states, "As soon as I stopped trying to think about a business idea and started focusing on what I'm passionate about, that's when it came to me." This was his lesson, and in sharing it, he is inspiring many would-be entrepreneurs to go for their passions.

The admired Walt Disney said, "Everyone falls down. Getting up is how you learn to walk." He faced a lot of criticism and failure in his first two business attempts. Later, he went on to create Disney Brothers' Studio. Today, The Walt Disney Company thrives as the world's largest independent media conglomerate in terms of revenue. But more importantly, the company expresses a spirit of imagination through theme parks, its signature character, Mickey Mouse, and family classic movies.

What do these innovators have in common? They did not let failure define them; they let it refine them and their ideas. Many entrepreneurs throw in the towel too soon, right before they reach a breakthrough moment, right before consumer popularity or an investor could lead them to success. Bouncing back from the brink of failure is a familiar narrative in business and commonplace for serial entrepreneurs. This kind of resilience is important for all of us.

People with resilient brains understand and embrace pain and failure and have the ability to get up, come back, and try again. They reframe disappointments into advantages, knowing any upset or letdown may be a new opportunity in disguise.

So, the next time you look at a problem, big or small, and catch yourself thinking, "I give up," consider that you are learning with each mistake. It is not about reaching some kind of end point, but learning a lesson along the way. If you think, "There's got to be a better way," ask, "What is the better way?"

And then proceed to find out how you might find that better way.

Learning Your Way to a Breakthrough

As soon as you learn a life lesson, the Universe will serve up a new situation that reflects the positive change inside of you. When you grow and change, life changes with you. The Universe always mirrors your internal landscape and serves up new situations when you are ready to experience them. The result can be a nice upgrade in life circumstances.

Doug, a client, had a job where his supervisor constantly criticized him. For a while, he felt trapped, upset, and anxious; but then he wondered: "What's the lesson here?" He owned it. As a student of life, he reflected on what his boss might be mirroring for him. Doug realized he had internalized a program of low self-worth from his supercritical and controlling mom. He decided to work on Wisdom Two – You Deserve Love. He focused on transforming from the inside out through emotional awareness and self-nurturing practices. Soon, he felt gratitude for the critical boss as the catalyst to become a more conscious and integrous person. In time, he applied for a better job with a social enterprise, and he got it. With a new sense of confidence, he worked with a dream team that valued him. Doug's new outer circumstances were a reflection of who he became and what he learned through his transformational healing.

Lessons show up in all areas of our life. We draw people and events to us, to learn what our soul yearns to learn. When it comes to finding and keeping love, lessons abound. For example, through dating, you get a better idea of what you want and what you don't want. When a relationship comes to an end, you take note of what didn't work and how you grew as a person in the process. With newly found insights, you are more discerning about the man or woman you date the next time. You are learning what to avoid and what to attract. Eventually, you find someone who is a lot closer to being Mr. or Ms. Right for you—you might even find "the one." Along the way, you become a better friend, lover, and partner. You grow in character traits like self-assurance and patience, too.

So, as a student of life, in all situations you can ask: "What am I learning?" "How am I becoming a better person?" And these inquiries help you to make course corrections. You then face the world with newly found strength, perspective, and insight. Isn't it remarkable how life serves up experiences perfectly suited for your growth? And, because you are living in a Benevolent Universe, you won't get more than you can handle.

How about embracing learning like developing and enjoying a new sport? Are you up for the challenge? As you become a committed player in the game of personal development, you are an inspiration to others in your humility and your triumphs. Don't you find pleasure in watching your friends and family grow and become better people? Isn't it inspiring to see athletes improve their skills? Aren't you more inclined to read a blog or watch a video that discloses the lessons learned through challenges, downturns, and turmoil—not just the high points?

We all recognize and admire the strength it takes to become a kinder, wiser, more aware person. We appreciate it when others admit to a wrong and learn from the misstep. We appreciate those who are real and relatable, not the "smarty pants" who touts their knowledge or success. We respect those who share growth from personal experience.

You've probably noticed that as you go through life you get similar lessons over and over again until you learn them. Girl, do I know that one! The characters will look different, but the lessons are the same. Over time, as you see the patterns, and if you evolve through your lessons, you'll do better. You won't make the same mistakes. At least, that is the goal with Wisdom Five – Learn as You Live. Learn in order to have a better life. Learn for the next time. (There will always be one.)

There is a Sufi anecdote about a proud mother who comes to the mullah (a wise and learned man) and boasts, "My son has learned all his lessons at the academy!" "Console yourself," says the mullah. "God will no doubt send him more."

Affirmations of Wisdom Five – Learn as You Live:

- I learn from every experience.
- I love to learn.
- I am evolving in consciousness.
- Life is my school house.
- The more I play, the more I learn.
- I am a student of life.

When Success Is a Verb

There are always more lessons to learn, more metaphoric (and sometimes actual) mountains to climb. But instead of feeling overwhelmed by the goal, straining to keep your eyes on the destination, what about shifting the focus? Instead of focusing on success—the destination, the place to go, the something to have—why not focus on the process of getting there? I like to call that process "successing"—it's a celebratory, "in-the-moment" way of moving forward in life. When you see success as a verb, it relieves the stress of pushing for the end result. You focus more on the process and your core values than the grip of the win-lose-success paradigm. This opens you to enjoy learning.

To say, "I am successing" means I am on a journey, and I am paying attention to where I am and who I am becoming as I am on my way somewhere (to reach a goal.)

Successing is living in alignment with your values. You are successing if you are supporting yourself as you walk the path—present to how you feel and what you are learning.

When you focus on the journey—the *who* you are becoming—you realize that the end result is not really the goal. The goal is the learning and the evolution. Truth be told, we measure success by the lessons we learn, the people we meet, who we become, and the joys of the doing. That is the satisfaction we are after—not the prize, medal, trophy, or reward. As we unlearn some of the socioeconomic success paradigms and family-of-origin ways of measuring achievement, we understand successing as a way of being.

Laurie Bagley, author of *Summit*, exemplified "successing" as she trained to climb Mount Everest. Her primary focus was not on the mountain peak; it was on attempting the climb—yes, doing all the training needed—but not obsessed with reaching the top of Everest. Laurie didn't want the pressure or seduction that comes from an all-consuming goal. She wanted to do the climb, inspire others, raise money for a humanitarian cause, and, most importantly, return home healthy to her daughter and community. So, she committed that during her ascent, she would turn back if she perceived a red flag. She would stay hyperalert to anything that would endanger her life. Hers was a different way of looking at goal-setting and success. She was in for the climb not only to reach the summit. As fate had it, she did make it to the top and became the sixth U.S. woman to summit Mount Everest from the North Col route.

Laurie says, "You don't have to reach for success; it's already here. It's in how you live." This is when success is a verb. And when success is a verb you always win, while you take care of yourself along the way.

Letting Life Teach You

LIFE is a process.

Life's experiences are our coursework in the school of life. However, not every subject is easy! Sometimes getting kicked in the butt is what it takes to move us forward on our journey. An easy lesson might be something like driving too fast on a country road, and getting pulled over by the town cop. He sees that you are a local and lets you off with a lecture and a warning. Now, if you learned your lesson, you are going to drive more slowly and carefully in order not to be a hazard to yourself and others. If you didn't learn your lesson, you might continue to speed and eventually get a ticket and a fine. Or worse yet, you could have an accident.

So, like a warning from a cop, the Universe will warn you, too. Sometimes it feels a bit like a cosmic joke. If you pay enough attention, you'll start getting your warnings more quickly and avoid the "fines" (the harder lessons and tougher consequences). This is what happened to a friend of mine.

An avid hiker, Renee, headed out on the mountain to explore a new trail. She stashed in her backpack a bottle of water, a snack bar, an extra layer of clothes, and her cell phone. That was routine for her. While Renee had a general idea of the loop she was hoping to explore, she did not know the path; and as she hiked, the trail markers became less visible. Soon, she got lost. Eventually, she ended on a forest road far from the ridgetop landmark she hoped to find and even further from where she parked her car.

Disoriented, she spent more than four hours following forest roads, wandering astray amongst tall trees and brush, until she found a power line to hike beneath. She kept calm for the most part, but as she ran out of water and her legs let out with fatigue, she admits to having a momentary panic attack. At last, Renee approached a broader forest road and saw a truck parked in the distance. The truck owner told her that she was five miles from town.

Now, this is when I need to digress and explain that the very morning of this "lost-in-the-woods" experience, Renee told me about some of her new business colleagues. She was judgmental and prejudice as she labeled them, "hunters with guns and big trucks."

Well, guess who saved her in the woods that day? A hunter with a Ford F-350, fully stocked with a Weatherby Vanguard Rifle that proudly hung in the cab. His name was R.J., and he gave Renee a ride to town in his safe rig. The air-conditioned ride felt like heaven to exhausted and overheated Renee. She had no problem listening to him talk about hunting trips as they drove down the rocky gravel road to town. In fact, she asked a lot of questions.

So, what was the lesson for Renee? Well, taking a map and compass on her next hiking trip might be one. But the bigger lesson that life gave Renee was the opportunity to face her prejudice and see a stereotype in a different light. The very persona she had judged in the morning was her hero in late afternoon. Lesson learned.

"You are always in a conversation with life, and life talks to you so that you might make better choices the next time."

Similar to Wisdoms One and Three which ignite trust and guidance and affirm the symbolic nature of life, Wisdom Five teaches you to use the symbolism in order to learn.

I'm sure you can relate to Renee's lesson. You or someone close to you may have judged a certain type of person and later came to know, like, and trust that very type of person. If we really pay attention, eventually we will learn not to judge at all; we will see that everyone is doing his or her best. It is not our business to evaluate another's process. It is rather, our honor and our lesson to accept people for who they are.

Learning from Triggers

When you understand the power of the caring Universe to serve you up the lessons you need, the instructor you've been waiting for is standing right in front of you—it is the person or the event you are most reactive to. That interaction shows you—every time—that the way out is in.

As Shawn Mahsie, developer of "The Symmetry of Happiness Theory," puts it, "Whatever is upsetting you is actually holding your path to peace—100 percent of the time." The shift from pain to peace does not have to be random guesswork, and it does not require a lifetime of hard work.

Your commitment to learning can create a massive shift in the way you see and meet life's challenges. Inevitably, when you are in a difficult situation and you ask, "What is the lesson here?"

you'll find a profound answer. And in the honest exploration, you grow into a better version of you, and life changes in a positive direction. An African proverb reminds us, "Smooth seas do not make skillful sailors."

Our triggers hold the answers. If something upsets you, there is unfinished business inside of you, wanting your attention. As you commit to growth, your emotions will reveal where you are wavering, where you have a "charge," and, therefore, where you need to grow. Triggers point to the specific areas where you want healing.

So, what do I mean by a "trigger?" A trigger is any input that stirs you up inside and sets off a reaction. A fear trigger creates mild butterflies in the stomach or agonizing, gut-wrenching pain. Depending on you and the situation at hand, a trigger might crank up your anxiety or insecurity, ignite your anger, or send you into an emotional tailspin. Triggers might also intensify sadness or feed an illusion of loneliness. It is as if a lid on a pressure tap was opened and the feelings bottled up inside of you fizz up and spill over. Or think of a trigger as unlocking a gun loaded with bullets. The bullets are your painful feelings; and if the trigger is pressed, boom!—out comes your pain.

What does a trigger look like? A trigger might be a passing comment, a complaint aimed at you, a perceived criticism about something you did wrong (or something you did not do that you should have), or it might be a public insult or rejection. Let's say your friend makes a comment about how your outfit is inappropriate for an occasion. Well, if you are insecure about how you look, that small comment can set you off into a rage and result in a rude reaction, or it might be internalized within and lead you to stew in self-doubt and self-condemnation. Either way, the "I'm-not-attractive" trigger button has been pushed.

Any time we have an insecurity, we are vulnerable to a real or imagined attack. If we don't disclose our sensitive spots to the people we trust in our lives, they might poke at them without meaning, too. When we are ultra-sensitive to a particular childhood wound, we get triggered even when comments are light-hearted and minute. We sometimes misinterpret reality.

A trigger can also be less direct. The storyline of a book or movie might trigger you. Let's say you see a would-be heroine make a terrible mistake in love, which reminds you of how you blew it in your last relationship—thus, triggering regret or self-loathing. Or let's say you hear a song on the radio and you flash back to your high school prom, when the love of your life left you and broke your heart. Inadvertent triggers cause hurt, just as much as direct ones, when they hit your sore spots—your unresolved issues.

Triggers can show you where you need to grow and where there are lessons to be learned. What triggers you? What bothers you about others? What gets you unexpectedly angry, frustrated, or overwhelmed? These observations become your very own training grounds for personal evolution and emotional awareness. Once you notice the things that set you off the most, once you catch the themes, you stop blaming the people or circumstances around you and take responsibility for your growth. At your best, you see that every trigger is gifting you with a prescription for freedom. This does not mean you put up with abuse or excessive criticism from others. Not at all. Speak up or get out if you are being treated aggressively or being exploited in any way. That is the inner-honoring teaching of Wisdom Two. You deserve love.

When you are in supportive relationships, you have a choice to use triggers to grow together. You can share your trigger spots with the people you love so that they can help you heal them. Kirk and I refer to our emotional-chronic-pain points as "broken toes." For example, I know that any comment I make that suggests that Kirk is not contributing enough is like stepping on a broken toe; it hurts like nobody's business. And he knows that the slightest indication that my belly is bloated can rile me up into a fit. We are careful in order to heal them. We affirm our care for each other, giving room for each other to challenge the fears. I appreciate how Kirk contributes, and he admires my belly. Over time, the toes heal: Kirk feels like he is giving and worthy, and I feel loved for who I am, not how I look.

As you find the lessons within the triggers, you heal your pain. You realize that your reactivity comes from an old wound—likely a pattern that extends back into your childhood. Remember, on the journey to a soul inspired life, we are in the business of aborting old, outdated, and fearful programs and interference, while nurturing new stories of love.

"Once you notice the things that set you off the most, once you catch the themes, you stop blaming the people or circumstances around you and take responsibility for your growth."

So now, as the empowered, self-aware, soulful you, when you are triggered, you have a choice. Do you react? Or do you pause and take a moment to find a peaceful response? Do you take note and choose to go deeper, beyond the trigger, to find the root of the pain—the fearful parts of you that try to defend their position? Do you let yourself feel the pain and do you release it? When you let go (be it through shadow work, emotional, or otherwise), you de-charge yourself. Over time, when your old triggers reappear, you won't feel activated. The painful emotional charge that propelled the hurtful retaliations will have been defused.

Eckhart Tolle reminds us, "Life will give you whatever experience is most helpful for the evolution of your consciousness. How do you know this is the experience you need? Because this is the experience you are having at the moment."

Consequence Is a Great Teacher

Lessons arrive in our life as responses to our actions. Consequence is a great teacher. We know what is right and wrong. It's wrong to lie, steal, manipulate for gain, intentionally hurt another, exert power over another, gossip, and so on. When we trespass on our personal ethics (our integrity), there will be consequences. To varying degrees, we have all overstepped what we know to be "right" at some point in our lives. When we do this, we learn. We learn through the consequence, such as lost friendship, a financial fine, a court order, public shame, a lost job, and so forth.

When this happens to you, you may feel remorse, but I do not recommend holding on to regret. Let me explain. Remorse allows you to make amends, feel the pain, and commit to doing it differently next time. You take responsibility for the consequence and learn from it in order not to repeat it.

However, regret builds up more pain as it focuses on the terrible wrongdoing, the unchangeable past. Regret is often self-condemning. Regret holds on to self-pity, sadness, shame, and disappointment. Regret gets you stuck in the past.

Remorse gets you moving—considering how to compensate and correct. Remorse opens the way for forgiveness. Feeling remorse can be healthy, as long as you don't cling to the guilt that often accompanies it. Remorse reminds us to change, let go, and to act with more integrity the next time.

Expect Evolution

You will notice that life ebbs and flows. Do not be discouraged if you find yourself feeling down after a period of being up. This is natural. We feel wonderful—in the flow—happy and at ease, and then we crash and burn. We get hurt. We get angry. We let the triggers of life exaggerate our fears. This is part of the life journey; don't let anyone tell you otherwise.

When we are ruthlessly honest with ourselves, we see that our states of consciousness fluctuate. At one point, you might feel like you've aced a new concept, passed a cosmic test, or embodied a wisdom principle in a real-life situation. Good for you. But maybe the very next day you wish you could stay under the covers because life got hard and inner-honoring or gratitude were more than you could muster.

Here is the good news: Everything changes. Everything evolves. This is a universal truth. As you revisit your lessons regularly, you will stabilize your knowing—not your intellectual comprehension, but your deep, somatic knowing. You will understand something different each time. The most important advice is to be kind to yourself along the way.

Be present and accept the state of mind you find yourself in no matter what that "here" looks like. If you don't give up on yourself, you will be able to gain the strength and insight to move forward and be present for yourself and others. For more support, see the "Start Where You Are Affirmations" in the Appendix.

Re-center When You Stumble

Yes, just when you think you've found your way, a life challenge may show up and give you the opportunity to practice what you've learned. Are you solid in your newly found attributes?

When the rubber meets the road, are you in congruence with your yearning and actions? A life challenge serves as a check-in and will allow you to find your strength and/or course-correct, if you need to. Everyone stumbles and falls, especially when learning and practicing something new.

My client Lynette came to know this experience in her business. Lynette called me in a panic. A work situation had not turned out as she had hoped it would. Lynette had allowed a boss to manipulate her. "My employer took advantage of my dreams. He promised a lot of money (one of my most tempting distractions) and I took the bait. I was caught. I sold my soul for cash. I am miserable, confused, and anxious."

Lynette shared more of the particulars of her story—just enough to get me, her coach, oriented, and to see the situation from a bird's eye view.

I reminded her how the Universe mirrors our state of mind: "Fear is a contracting force. If you contract, the world contracts around you. As you become small-minded, the world changes to accommodate you. Your worry will be replicated in the events of outer world unless you re-center."

"No matter the problems in your life, a solution sits peacefully within you."

As I shared my observations, Lynette widened her perspective enough to get out of her own way, out of her part in the drama, and into an observer mindset. This kind of shift of perspective is not easy, which is why honest friends, counselors, and coaches are indispensable when times are hard.

I continued, "When your boss transgresses in a demanding way, and tells you what you should believe, watch without reaction. Make assessments. If the intrusion is more than what you can handle, you can leave. You are not serving a life sentence. In the meantime, while you work with this company, be clear-minded and continually re-center."

Taking in this message, Lynette began to feel a bit more relaxed.

In this process, I met Lynette where she was. We started with naming the situation and the fear. I did not push her toward any premature decisions. I walked with her through gradual realizations. We started with her pain; and over time, Lynette arrived in a new place: a place of empowerment.

I told her what my teacher David had taught me, "Re-center continually. It is not how many times you leave that matters. It is how many times you return. That is the mastery—the constant return."

Over the next months, Lynette was re-centering and making gradual adjustments. Over time, she left the job and found other employment that built her confidence. She re-committed to following her dreams, pledging to be true to her values and intuition, and to not following the lure of money.

Like Lynette, we all fall into traps. There are many lures that can hook us and take us off track and out of integrity with our soul. This is where guidance can come to the rescue. As suggested in Wisdom Three, investigate what blind spots you may have (fears and desires), so you don't detour from your soul path. Let life guide you to your potential. (That is its job.)

You can maintain your center in the midst of all of life's challenges. Just know situations will challenge you; it is supposed to be that way. But always know that whatever happens is for the good and look for the lessons. Be in the eye of the hurricane.

No matter the problems in your life, a solution sits peacefully within you. Your life will unfold correctly if you don't contract into fear. You need every experience on your life journey. The trick is to be okay with where you are and not to be afraid of moving to a better place. There is always a better place waiting for you. You just need to course-correct your inner landscape and find the sweet spot of peace within. Soon the Universe will recalibrate according to that vibration and show the way to a better place. When you are at peace, you attract better solutions. You resonate with a peace-giving field of possibility.

Proactive Learning

You can let life teach you what you need to know; you can also be proactive in your learning.

Some inspired ways to seek out learning include:
- Choosing yearly themes
- Creating "successing" pledges
- Seeking out good company
- Taking bold steps toward your growth

Choose a yearly theme for learning and see how the Universe responds. Every New Year's Eve for about a decade now, I have chosen a theme for the year—the area I most want to study and understand in the months ahead. This is different from new year's resolutions because learning themes focus on new understandings more than accomplishments and forced outer changes.

The theme helps me choose learning tools, such as books and retreats, and select experiences that will help me learn the theme I have chosen to study in a deeply embodied way. I always marvel at the way the Universe contributes to my evolving. All year, I hold the intention to better understand and grow in a new area.

Here are a few examples:

- *Let thy will and my will be one*: The year that I started to see the vision of a personal development company.
- *Intuition:* The year I followed a hunch and went to Hawaii, which is where I found deep healing and renewal.
- *Courage:* The year that I had the courage to do nothing... a new pattern for the "busy me."
- *To be a conduit of the Divine:* The year I started writing and was asked to do more public speaking.
- *Love and Relationships:* The year Kirk and I fell in love.

Create pledges to support the idea of "successing." As discussed earlier in this Wisdom, successing is about who you become as you are accomplishing your goals. Making pledges to yourself helps you focus on the process, rather than concentrating on the all-consuming push to a finish line (or the top of a mountain.)

Personal pledges offer clarity to remind you of the importance of whole-hearted living, instead of pressing a pause button until some goal is achieved. Pledges are meant to be reviewed regularly and not stashed away; they trump the goals. You never go for the goal at the cost of your personal pledge.

Here are some examples of personal pledges that support successing:

- In the process of losing weight, you could say: "I let go of ten pounds through healthy exercise, balanced eating, and nourishing rest."
- When your company is encouraging greater sales and you are putting together an action plan, you could pledge, "I maintain a balanced life, and act in integrity as I achieve my sales goals."

- When you are seeking greater closeness in a relationship, whether it's friendship, family, or marriage—you could say: "I am happy to be building a close relationship with (fill in the blank) and being true to myself in the process." How can you be true to someone else if you are not true to yourself?

Not long ago, I worked through a pledge of my own: I enjoy biking and I had set a goal to complete a 100-mile bike ride. I rode longer and longer distances to get closer to my goal, and I would come back with a backache. So, I made a pledge that achieving a century ride was not as important as my spinal health. I sought out a Pilates instructor and started exercising to strengthen my core and my spine. This was an absolute shift in intention. Because of that personal pledge, I learned that what was more important to me than the 100-mile biking goal was my health and my spine.

There may be a day when I will bike a century, but only if I know that I will get off my bike and my back will feel wonderful.

Seek out the good company of others. One of the most reliable learning tactics is seeking out mentors and teachers. We are blessed to be able to learn through others. Early in my life, I got the sense that I ought to listen to the people whom I admired and follow their lead. After all, I wanted to emulate their strengths—be it their beauty, athletic abilities, intelligence, or spiritual awareness. So, whenever I set a new intention or goal, I find someone who is already where I want to be and learn from them.

When I wanted to summit Mount Shasta, I asked Laurie, who had summited Mount Everest, to help me. For three months, we met every week to train, and we climbed surrounding peaks and steep ridges. Spending time in her "can-do" presence, I caught a "can-do" attitude. Yes, I stretched my limits and followed her specific guidance on preparation. Her confidence was infectious and fed mine. I reached Mount Shasta's 14,180-foot peak on June 1, 2001. It remains a highlight of my life.

I would have never achieved this massive feat without Laurie's help and companionship. I know that I did the wisest thing I could have done. I knew where I wanted to go, and I found someone who had been there before.

Be in the good company of those who inspire you. Celebrate their inspiration. While jealousy may kick in, do your best to dismiss any tendency to compare yourself to them. Stop those competitive thoughts as quickly as they come. Instead, feel the inspiration of being with people who are accomplished in their fields and bask in that delight. Learn to be enthused for them. Admire their bright genius and know you can reach your potential too—if that's what you wish and if you apply yourself. Your merriment will build a resonance that will allow you to become what you desire and attract more of the same.

My definition of good company also includes the company of books, movies, videos, podcasts, activities, and music. Good company includes all of the inputs in life. I have learned to find mentors, coaches, trainers, and guides. I encourage you to do the same. In Sanskrit, a word for good company is "satsang." It is not only the fastest track to climbing mountains, but according to Hindu tradition, it is also the key to achieving enlightenment. When one spiritual guru was asked by a devotee, "How can I reach enlightenment?" The teacher answered, "Satsang. Good company."

In the Appendix, you can take a "good company" assessment. You'll be led to develop your inventory of influences, and you'll rate how each influence gives you energy or takes it away. With new awareness, you are invited to make alterations and create change.

In Proverbs 13:20, Solomon wrote: "He that walketh with wise men shall be wise: but a companion of fools shall be destroyed." Who you spend your time with, what you watch, read, and listen to, the places you frequent, and the activities you do, all predict your future. If you want to have more money, spend time with people with money. If partnership is what you are after, spend more time with couples. If you want to become a soul inspired person, attend personal development workshops. We learn by examples and from positive influences.

My teacher David tells the story of a great sage who bestowed blessings on those who came to him for healing. In his good company and through his prayers, people received miraculous transformations of mind, body, and spirit.

> One day a student of this sage wanted to know how he prepared for the healings. So, he hid in the healer's closet. From this hidden spot, he heard the sage reciting a great spiritual teaching. An emotionally afflicted seeker came in for a blessing and left with all her sorrow erased.
>
> Then the sage said, 'You can come out of the closet now.' A sensitive man, he knew his student was hiding there.
>
> The sage continued, 'The reason I recite the great teachings is because the power within the phrases transmits the energy I need in order for me to bless others. As I learn, I tap into a wisdom greater than myself. Within the best of teachings and scriptures, there is a profound, transformational power infused into the words. It is this healing power that I transmit to others.'

Take bold steps toward your growth. Wisdom Four – Take Inspired Action, gives us permission to take risks so we can live life to the fullest. When we do this we open ourselves to Wisdom Five – Learn as You Live, as the following example illustrates.

In 2008, I was hired by an economic development nonprofit to teach a course on entrepreneurship, specifically business planning. I had never taught a college course before. And while I had started and built three successful small businesses, I'd never formally studied business. As much as I felt the calling to teach the course, I also doubted my academic credentials.

I told the class that we were going to have some fun exploring the schoolbook way to build a business, and we'd do it together. I assured them that this spirit of adventure is exactly what it takes to become an entrepreneur! Starting and succeeding in business requires accomplishing a series of tasks that involve figuring things out as you go. (It also requires a lot of positive belief.)

I disclosed my insecurities to the students—and, as a result, I think I also inadvertently expressed my confidence and genuine desire to help. I shared that I had not personally completed a long-form, loan-ready business plan for any of my businesses.

The class valued my honesty. We investigated our way through business planning, market research, cash-flow projections, bookkeeping, and marketing strategies. Everyone grew in the collective innocence and spirit of newness and the deep dive into the best academic practices.

Who would have guessed the outcome? More than ten years later, I thrive in the subject of business planning. But in every course that I have taught since that first one, I share the truth that success comes from figuring things out as you go along. From this experience, I no longer seek out the perfect-looking trainers or teachers. I no longer try to be one, either. I prefer the teachers who are not afraid of revealing their Achilles' heel. I love to learn from companion guides who understand the process of forever mastering—forever becoming.

Learn to Love to Learn

Expansion and evolution are the very nature of the Universe. Our planet undergoes continual change, adaptation, and evolution. Humans don't only evolve physically or as species,

we also evolve in consciousness. We are evolving collectively. We are on a progressive journey in life.

Klaus Schwab, the founder and executive chairman of the World Economic Forum and cofounder of the Schwab Foundation for Social Entrepreneurship, has noted: "Change can be frightening, and the temptation is often to resist. But change almost always provides opportunities to learn new things, to rethink tired processes, and to improve the way we work." Change also improves the way we live and love.

Learning does not stop. You learn and evolve throughout your life whether you like it or not. However, you can speed up the pace and let it be easier when you allow it, look forward to it, and learn to love to learn. Learning becomes fun when you let go of resistance and trust life. You may stumble and fall, explore and examine, but to do nothing is to stagnate.

When we choose to learn and evolve, we ask a lot of questions. It's a great pleasure to get the mind churning, the images appearing, and the juices flowing. When we ponder, we often find answers within. When we open, we see the way.

But it is never fully "the way" until we walk it, grok it, and make it our own. We must embody it. Your mission, if you choose to accept it, is to embody what you learn. Take it in fully, and let that embrace fill your every cell. With the embodiment of new lessons, your life will transform, and your soul will evolve.

Welcome to Evolving Learn as You Live. You become
self-aware in order to learn and grow. There is no trip as epic as the journey of expanding consciousness.

Gems for the Journey

- The Fifth Wisdom is Learn as You Live. Life is for learning. As you commit to a soul inspired life, you experiment and you evolve.
- When you are a student of life, no matter what happens, you are learning and growing. This means you don't have to be perfect. This means you don't have to be right. This means things can go well or not go so well, but either way you'll learn something.
- Life's circumstances are your lessons in the school of life. Not every subject is easy! Your triggers are your teachers. When you are open minded, you will embrace the discovery.

Walking with the Wisdoms

- The next time something goes other than the way you hoped, ask yourself, "What can I learn from this?" The next time you are triggered, ask yourself, "What is this teaching me about myself?"
- Find an area of life where you'd like to grow and learn. Learn in the way that brings you joy. Research the topic online, take a class, attend an event on the subject, practice the new skill, find a mentor, or read a book by someone who knows the topic or has had the experience you are wondering about. Fill out the "Good Company Assessment" in the Appendix.

- Make a commitment to yourself to change your attitude about success. Prioritize the learning process, not the end point, and say, "I am successing. I'm on my way." Develop a successing statement and personal pledge that focuses on who you are being (or becoming) in the process.
- Download the "Two-Minute Evolving Activation" at: *www.ASoulInspiredLife.com/wisdoms*

Inner-Views for Journaling and Conversations

These are sentence stems that you are encouraged to complete and elaborate on. Take your time and see where your writing goes or how a conversation unfolds.

- What learning means to me is . . .
- Evolving is . . .
- I'm proud of myself for learning . . .
- The area I most want to grow in is . . .
- A mistake I've made is . . . and what I've learned from that mistake is . . .
- One of my triggers is . . .and what it is showing me is . . .
- Someone I will reach out to and learn from is . . .

Pause and Remember:

- Life Is for You
- You Deserve Love
- Life Is Guiding You
- Take Inspired Action
- Learn as You Live

If Truth Comes Humbly

My teachers are the flowers
and the organic matter in the soil.

My champions are loving mothers,
engaged fathers, and day-care providers.

My mentors are the patient monks and nuns,
the happily married, and the children that laugh at themselves.

My wisdom comes from crawling creatures,
water worn sea shells, and the passing clouds.

My lessons are the embarrassing moments,
the tears, and the apologies.

My growth is through gifts of the heart,
home-cooked meals, and warm hugs.

If truth comes humbly,
then make my teachers the soft at heart.

WISDOM

6

Choose Gratitude

*"We think we have to do something to be grateful,
or something has to be done in order for us to be grateful,
when gratitude is a state of being."*

—IYANLA VANZANT

American Author, Speaker, Teacher, Television Personality

The Wisdoms continue to build on themselves with the renewing energy of gratitude. With this Wisdom, you appreciate life in all its wonder and mystery—feeling awe within yourself and expressing it to others. Anyone who sincerely feels gratitude understands its power. Gratitude can transform a humdrum day into a celebration, shift negative thinking into a positive direction, and infuse your life with enthusiasm and joy. It anchors you into the possibility of the present moment. You realize what a gift it is to be alive and become more mindful of how you live, love, and lead. It's as if you have new eyes to see what might have gone unnoticed before.

"Gratitude can transform a humdrum day into a celebration, shift negative thinking into a positive direction, and infuse your life with enthusiasm and joy."

Most of all, gratitude reminds you not to take people, experiences, your good fortune, and all the other elements of your life for granted. As Sarah Ban Breathnach, who brought gratitude to popular attention with her 1995 book, *Simple Abundance*, says: "You simply will not be the same person two months from now after consciously giving thanks each day for the abundance that exists in your life. And you will have set in motion an ancient spiritual law: The more you are grateful for what you've been given, the more will be given you."

Cultivating an Attitude of Gratitude

LOVE BLOSSOMS IN MANY FORMS. ALL ARE BEAUTIFUL.

Gratitude blossoms organically when your soul is the soil of your life, that which nurtures and feeds you. As stated in earlier chapters, personality-driven goals don't bring you sustainable happiness, but your soul inspired thoughts and expressions do. And in that happiness, you think thoughts and speak words like, "Thank you." "I am so blessed." And "I appreciate you."

As much as we buy into the erroneous social programming, that events or things in the outside world will bring us the inner peace and happiness we are looking for, and as much as we chase after shiny objects, we won't experience sustainable happiness until we release the cultural programming that misleads us into looking for happiness on the outside, and make the shift to choose gratitude and appreciate what is in our life right now.

When you let go of trying to buy your way to happiness, you find your true nature of ease, connection, and enthusiasm—your soul self. As Marci Shimoff writes, "You don't have to win the lottery or lose twenty pounds . . . what you put your attention on grows stronger in your life. Put your attention on happiness by practicing happiness habits each day." What you appreciate, appreciates. Gratitude is a happiness habit.

Attributes of Wisdom Six – Choose Gratitude:

- Appreciative
- Thankful
- Grateful
- Content
- Enthusiastic
- Happy

Gratitude as a Practice

A practice of gratitude is the simplest way to a happier life—a more soul inspired life with honest, loving relationships. When you focus your attention on what is going right, you turn the tide toward positivity. Inevitably your mood lifts. You can start the ball rolling. Nothing needs to happen for you to be grateful; you can adopt an attitude of gratitude and you will find more things to be grateful for in your life. Take the initiative to turn your antenna to the positive.

Perhaps you already have a gratitude practice—a mental list you review regularly or a list you write down every day in a notebook or journal. That list undoubtedly shifts daily as you interact with people, experience a variety of events, and notice the renewed beauty of life around you. Especially on the days when you are feeling gloomy, it is essential to choose gratitude because when you focus on what you are thankful for, there is less room—maybe no room—for negative thoughts or complaints. There is always something you can be grateful for—sunshine, an animal, a tree, the laughter of a child, a warm cup of coffee, or a smile that comes your way.

When you find yourself dissatisfied with an aspect of your life, find something to appreciate. For example, instead of fretting about a stain on your shirt or a facial blemish; focus on the fact you have the means to own clothes and be thankful for the good health and beauty features that you do have. When you are upset with something that is not going right at work, be grateful for the resources your job provides or the parts of your job you do enjoy.

Jean-Baptiste Alphonse Karr, a French critic, journalist, and novelist, wrote, "Some people grumble that roses have thorns. I am grateful that thorns have roses." If you don't like the thoughts you are thinking, change the playlist of your thoughts and shift to gratitude. The more you train yourself to shift your thinking away from what you don't have to what you do have, the more you will get in sync with this Wisdom and revel in the life you are living.

If you've taken to heart the Wisdoms that precede gratitude, you've come to understand that there is always a silver lining in any unfortunate or problematic situation. Can you give thanks for the petty tyrants in your life? When you appreciate a "rock in your shoe" as the catalyst you need to look at an aspect of yourself, change, and grow, you find yourself in a state of gratitude. Yes, the process may feel "challenging," but you can give thanks that you are, indeed, growing and evolving.

Expressing gratitude does not mean that you deny what needs fixing in yourself, your life, and in the world around you. Nor does gratitude give you permission to polish over hurts and disappointments in a form of spiritual bypass. Instead, give thanks for the situation, the challenge, and take aligned action from a place of passion—not anger or fear. It can be as simple as saying to yourself, "Thank you for this lesson." Then proceed with making any necessary changes—your sacred activism, conflict resolution, and compassionate communication. With gratitude for your lessons, you make changes with a deeper sense of peace.

Tony Robbins states, "Gratitude is the antidote to the things that mess us up. You can't be angry and grateful simultaneously. You can't be fearful and grateful simultaneously. So, gratitude is the solution to both anger and fear."

You come alive with gratitude. Aliveness of spirit is a natural by-product. You are not forcing yourself into anything. You are simply asking an empowering question, "Right now, what am I grateful for?" In any moment, there will be an answer, and another, and another—if you ask. And with the momentum of giving thanks, you find yourself in an entirely new state of mind. A positive one. Soon, a smile crosses your face, you feel warmth in your heart; something has shifted.

Happiness and contentment from within will allow you to express yourself with love towards others and fuel your artistic and creative endeavors in the world. My teacher David explains: "The Divine presence is looking for a window to come through. It is your happiness that is that window." Gratitude is all about becoming the window that lets inspiration in and through you.

Gratitude Attracts Benevolence

Gratitude can set in motion the spiritual law of attraction in unexpected and light-hearted ways.

Two of my friends Robert and Bonnie drove through Mt. Shasta and stopped by for a visit. I've always admired them for their Midas touch. It seems everything they worked on or invested in turned to gold. We had been business partners in the past, and I had benefited from their good luck. Or was it really luck after all?

As Robert, Bonnie, and I hiked along the flowing waters in a gorgeous alpine meadow, I inquired about their ease at manifesting abundance. Bonnie shared: "I love money. I love what I can do with it. I appreciate all the money we've made and hope to make more. What I especially appreciate is sharing it with others."

Just then, we approached a small bend in the path. Bonnie, who was in the lead, bent down to pick something up. She was laughing as she rose. Then, Bonnie turned around, faced Robert and me, and flashed fifty dollars in the air—two twenty-dollar bills and one ten. Awestruck, I was delighted to see this instant manifestation of what we were just talking about. Bonnie loves money, and money loves her. Bonnie smiled and handed Robert and me each a twenty-dollar bill. She kept the ten. We took a selfie to capture the moment, and I took an inner pause to capture the real-life example of the power of gratitude. I'll never forget this experience of manifestation. The Universe is so kind. And it has a sense of humor too! As a side note, I later donated that twenty-dollars to the meadow restoration program, giving it back to where it was found.

How well you manage your blessings matters, too. A person who appreciates, as opposed to someone who takes stuff for granted, is the person who is more inclined to manage accounts, possessions, and gifts carefully.

Just imagine a child with two scoops of ice cream on a sugar cone. If he is careless and obsessed with licking up the treat as fast as possible, he might lose the balance of the two scoops. One might drop. Let's say he does drop the ice cream. Now imagine that little boy asking his parent for a replacement, but this time he wants three scoops. A loving and wise parent might think, "He can't even handle two, why would I give him three?"

It's the same with the Benevolent Universe, which is energetically with you, noticing if you appreciate and take care of what you do have, before you get more. Your appreciation can apply to your health, talents, relationships, and the things you collect. Are you putting appreciation in action by maintaining, nurturing, and bettering your innate gifts as well as your material possessions? Specifically, do you maintain your car? Is your home clear of clutter? Are your financial books in order, and are your bills paid on time?

And when you do pay a bill, I recommend that you feel gratitude for the ability to pay it. This is something I started doing in my early twenties. Elated that I could live independently, I gave thanks as I wrote my first checks. This habit continues to this day. As I pay for purchases, I think, "I am grateful that I can afford this. Thank you."

"Gratitude can set in motion the spiritual law of attraction in unexpected and light-hearted ways."

Gratitude as Prayer

It's been said by many Wisdom Warriors that gratitude is a form of prayer. The thirteenth-century theologian and mystic Meister Eckhart noted: "If the only prayer you said in your whole life was 'thank you,' that would be enough."

When you are in the prayerful state of gratitude, you are not asking for what you think you want, you are giving thanks for what you have now and what you know is coming to you from the Benevolent Universe. Even when you are experiencing something difficult, as you've already learned, the silver lining— the lesson—is just what you need to turn your situation around and perhaps course-correct your life. So, the next time be grateful for the challenge, and say, "Thank you for the lesson." With gratitude, you can emphasize an appreciation for Wisdom Five–Learn as You Live. Try it, "Thank you for the lessons I am learning." How does that feel?

When I was growing up, my beautiful grandmother used to tell me, "Every thought is a prayer, and ever prayer is a thought." A loving being, rooted in faith, I enjoyed spending time with her, listening to what she had to say. Nonie, as we called her, is part of why I dare to live an intentional life. Based on her counsel, I make the everyday more sacred.

If you know that the energy of the Universe is mirroring your feelings, and lining up experiences based on your thoughts and deeds imagine how life could be if you choose to be rooted in a prayerful state of gratitude.

Prayer is communion from the heart. When I pray, I don't know what I'm going to say until I say it. I find the more that I am relaxed, the more words simply flow like water, like a river, like a fountain. And when there is nothing to be said, there is stillness.

Engaging in artistic projects and creating original music, poetry, and other works can also be seen as times of prayer. As many grateful creators have reported, the ego seems to drop away, and Divine Intelligence moves in and through. This is true inspiration at play.

Pray for The Highest Good

When we pray for our friends' or our family's well-being, or for those who are suffering, we open our hearts and access our compassion. However, I believe it's important not to second-guess what they might need—not to pray for a specific result—but, instead, to pray for others' highest good to unfold, to wish for what's best for each individual soul's journey. We are unlikely to know the lessons and experiences necessary for each person's growth. But we can pray that they learn their lessons with ease and grace. We can ask that Divine Will be done. As stated in Wisdom One, you can let go of any desire to manipulate the outcome and allow the greater good and the cosmic justice system to take its course. What you can pray for is others' ability to find peace in the situation they are in. You can pray in gratitude for their presence in your life. This sends a very positive, genuine vibration across the quantum field.

When you pray for yourself, the stance can be the same: "Thy will be done." Trust that you are receiving what you need. Rest assured, you may not get what you think you want, but you will get what you need. Be sure to add a "thank you." This is praying with gratitude.

I once read a story about a man who healed himself of an illness through gratitude. He was sick with pneumonia, and he cured himself through prayer. What did he pray? "Thank you God for all the blessings I've received in my life and thank you for all the blessings I will receive." Over a period of twenty-four hours, he wrote this statement in longhand, spoke it into a tape recorder, and repeated it over and over constantly. This indeed is a simple prayer that anyone can continually offer. Miracles are sure to follow.

Affirmations of Wisdom Six – Choose Gratitude:

- I am grateful for my life.
- Thank you, everything.
- What I appreciate, appreciates.
- It is my joy to appreciate others.
- I am blessed.
- I see beauty every day in many ways.

If you like to pray to music, I recommend Olivia Newton-John's acclaimed album, *Grace and Gratitude*. The lyrics blend her original inspirations with multi-traditional chants and spiritual prayers. I feel uplifted when I listen and sing along.

If you attend one of Olivia's concerts or buy one of her more recent CDs, you'll hear songs that encourage strength, and you'll feel her voice oozing care and contentment. She is quoted as saying, "I love my life, and nothing intimidates me anymore," and, "You never know what the future holds, so I am just enjoying being happy and healthy, and I feel grateful to have my wonderful husband by my side." Olivia also extends her gratitude by giving to others. She has created the "Olivia Newton-John Cancer Wellness and Research Centre" in her native country—Australia. In the centre, gratitude is a part of a holistic program for healing.

When you make gratitude an ongoing part of your life, the energy of gratitude is far more potent than the words you speak.

You pray, sing, and move with a full heart and allow the magic of prayer to move through you. The flavor of what I often pray might be expressed along these lines:

Thank you for the blessings in every opportunity.
Show me the way.
Thank you for the gifts in everything that happens to me.
Let me see the good.

My dear friend and hiking partner, Mary, and I share a regular gratitude prayer practice. For several years now, we've incorporated a quarterly ceremony into our Gateway climbs. On the winter and summer solstices and the spring and fall equinoxes, we make a point to wander a bit farther up from our usual trail route to what we now call our "special circle sanctuary." We offer gratitude prayers in the woods. We alternate speaking our prayers out loud while the other holds witness, and we celebrate what has transpired in the preceding three months. We honor and applaud our lessons learned and are grateful for the many gifts we have received. Mary and I also give thanks for what is to come. We recognize good is coming our way in the new season ahead.

Praying with another magnifies the power and presence of love and appreciation. My mom and I started a tradition years ago, called, "Moments in Time." Our first moment in time happened when we were in nature without a camera. As much as we wanted to take a photo to record the stunning scenery, we couldn't. We chose to capture the precious moment in the "emulsion of our minds." Now, with or without a camera on hand, we often stop when we are enjoying a special instance together, and say, "This is a Moment in Time." We pause to appreciate it, record it in our memory, savor the sweetness, and give thanks.

When asked about their gratitude practice, my friends, colleagues and clients said:

- "The very first thing I do in the morning is to offer gratitude. It sets up the energetics for the day."
- "Every night at bedtime I give thanks for five things from the day. This helps with insomnia because worries drop away and good feelings emerge."
- "We do a gratitude sharing before dinner as a family—holding hands and listening to each other."
- "When I lie down to sleep, I put my hand on my heart and express gratitude for whatever comes to mind."

Giving Gratitude

It is one thing to be in a state of gratitude and express your appreciation to the Universe internally, in writing, or out loud. It is something else to express the positive emotion of gratitude to another person. As Pulitzer-Prize winning poet, Edwin Arlington Robinson, once said: "There are two kinds of gratitude—the kind we feel for what we've been given, but the larger kind is for what we give."

Giving gratitude to another person can change not only your day, but their day too. It's an incredible gift that does not cost anything. When it's sincere, giving gratitude feels fantastic. Have you noticed how you feel after you give a compliment? Really happy! And chances are, so does the recipient.

In fact, one of the keys to happy relationships is genuine appreciation. In the "Lasting Love Connection" program that I offer, I promote appreciation as an essential communication skill in building a safe and secure zone in relationships. Appreciations work for children, friends, and co-workers too.

I want to express my gratitude to Dr. Warren Farrell for the insights that follow. Dr. Farrell mentored Kirk and me in

"The Art and Discipline of Love"™. He is the one who got us started in the relationship field and taught us about the power of appreciations and how to give meaningful appreciations.

How to Appreciate Others

The best appreciations are specific. Speaking in generalities is not as personal and intimate as describing something specific about someone or something that you appreciate. You could say "You look nice," but expressing, "I really love the way you brushed your hair tonight and how you ironed your shirt. You look amazing!" This is a more specific appreciation. Instead of saying, "Dinner is good. Thank you," which is rather lukewarm, how about describing what you love about the meal? "Wow, the spices in the curry sauce are perfect." Or, "I really like the selection of veggies, and they are a little crisp—just how I like them."

In a work situation, instead of a simple, "Thanks for your help," you might say, "I really appreciate your attention to detail in editing my report and how you enhanced the graphics."

Appreciations that are specific impress the ones receiving them because they know the appreciation is meant for them and comes from your heart. They will know that your comment is not canned and that you mean what you say. They feel noticed.

Appreciate often. Indulge in letting your loved ones know how much you care about them. Let them know what you truly love about them. Three specific appreciations a day is not too many. Perhaps you can share one appreciation in the morning, one mid-day, and one at night in a text message, email, over the phone, or in person. Any way and every day, appreciate. Make this a discipline and watch your friendships and your love life thrive. The more we are appreciated, the sweeter and more open we all become. Intimacy grows and hearts open.

With strangers or in business transactions, too, you might get into a habit of making appreciations an ongoing activity. An example, "Thanks for being such an attentive waiter." If this is new to you, I recommend setting an alert on your phone, at least once a day, to remind you to appreciate someone. You may also consider sending a card once a week to express some type of thank you.

Be creative when you appreciate. Perhaps you can leave a note on your spouse's pillow appreciating something specific about your beautiful love-making. Put a note on the counter, thanking someone in the family for doing the dishes. Write an appreciation poem. Draw a picture. Print a photo and scribble a love message on it. Make a short appreciation video. There is no creative limit to how you can express your appreciation. But the extra time you spend and the little bit of inspired creativity, goes a long way to making someone feel special. And it stretches you a bit too, which is the way of soul inspired living. Imagine coming home after a long day and seeing a tea-light candle with a love note on each step of the stairway leading up to your room. Would that romantic appreciation catch your attention? Of course, it would.

Appreciate when it's least expected. We all like happy surprises. Hide an appreciation note in your child's lunchbox for them to find later. Stick a card in your spouse's luggage. Appreciate your entire work team with a beautiful bouquet and card and display it in the breakroom. If you want to really surprise someone, appreciate them in the middle of a disagreement. You might say, "I'm really appreciating that you care about this topic. And by the way, you are really good at arguing." It might be just the pause you need to shift the energy toward conflict resolution.

Watch how positive acknowledgments change energy. When asked, "How was your day?" you could answer, "The best part is coming home to you." Don't get into a predictable appreciation rut, though; surprise and dazzle your partner and friends with random gratitude offerings.

Appreciate your people in ways that they like. Although the golden rule is, "Do unto others as you would have them do unto you," the platinum rule is, "Do unto others as they would have done unto themselves." If you know the people in your life well, you can come up with lots of custom-fit ways to share appreciation. Believe me, they not only will be touched but they also will feel understood. If your son likes Facebook messages, deliver your appreciation in that medium. If your mom likes a phone call in the mornings, call her.

In his book, *The Five Languages of Love*, Gary Chapman discusses the five major emotional languages that people "speak" and use to appreciate. In an intimate partnership, especially, you will want to find out how your lover likes to be acknowledged and loved. If gifts make him happy, buy or make gifts. If she appreciates words of affirmation, be sure you let her know how you feel about her through compliments, verbal support, and frequent communication by phone, email, and texting. Some people feel loved when they get help with tasks or chores. Others enjoy physical touch (including, but in addition to sex), or spending quality time together. If you aren't sure what language of love your loved ones speak, ask them, "How can I best appreciate you?" Then serve your love and gratitude in the flavor they most appreciate. You can take the Love Language quiz online at: *www.5lovelanguages.com*

Now that we've covered uplifting nuances of giving appreciations, let's discuss some of the important benefits of appreciations. The people in your life can change through the simple act of appreciating. Have you noticed that when you catch dogs doing something right and reward them, they do more of that behavior? This is dog training 101. It works on humans, too. We like it when someone notices and compliments us on a behavior change or good act. Most people feel a sense of pleasure in being noticed or celebrated for a soul inspired deed. It is a wise person who delights the people in his or her life with the treat of appreciation. Make it a practice to catch the people in your life doing something right, and appreciate it.

If you are in an intimate relationship, listen up. Criticism spoils a relationship. It kills love. No one likes to be criticized or told what they are doing wrong. Complaining about the unmade bed, laundry on the floor, or the TV blasting will get you nowhere. But I'll tell you what will get you somewhere. When your partner makes the bed, by golly, get happy and lavish appreciation. Any deed that you see your partner doing that you like, let him or her know. They will do more of it. "Honey, wow, the house looks great. Thank you for vacuuming. That makes me so happy." And you might even throw in some affection.

Appreciation is an art and not a manipulation tactic. It must be sincere for it to improve a relationship. Kirk lets me know when I dress up and wear an essential oil that he likes. I get the hint and express my feminine glow more often. Kirk's approach is superior to a critical comment such as, "Why don't you ever dress up? You look like a slob." Take note, smart men and women—You will find yourself with the partner of your dreams if you continue to catch them doing things right and complimenting, appreciating, and giving them your specific messages of gratitude. "Honey, you look and smell delicious!"

As you get in the habit of catching others and appreciating them for doing things right, why not treat yourself with the same respect and notice when you follow through on your own commitments? Celebrate your own little successes. Practice inner-honoring and give yourself a pleasant gift, a kind affirmation, or an inner-honoring activity. (Remember Wisdom Two?).

Giving Gratitude

- to loved ones fosters intimacy and deeper sharing.

- to co-workers builds connection.

- to strangers can contribute to a better world.

- to yourself is positive self-talk that lights you up in order to inspire.

- to the Benevolent Universe ensures a reverence for life.

Both being in a state of gratitude and giving gratitude are contagious. Once you do it, others around you will, too. Watch— and pass along your attitude of gratitude.

Gratitude with the Company You Keep

Ride the joyous waves of appreciation with yourself and others. Surround yourself with grateful people. Does your community encourage you to grow, succeed, and share your gratitude? Look at your relationships and ask, "Are we connecting with complaints or gratitude? Is this relationship giving energy or taking it?" Have you heard the saying, "Misery loves company?" Guess what? Gratitude loves company too! So, which do you choose?

The choice is yours. Maybe you fear that others will not be as comfortable around you if you are extraordinary, happy, inspired, and grateful. Or you fear that others will be envious of you or that they will avoid you. What others think of you is none of your business. Besides, if you need to spend less time with some of the negative people in your life, there are many empowered new friends awaiting your entry into the gratitude club. These friends will not envy you, they will celebrate you.

One of the most important inner-moves you can make is to choose gratitude and share it with others. By making conscious commitments with current or new friends, to celebrate each other and focus on what is good in your lives, you avoid the easy tendency to feel close only through troubles. As you do this, you grow in gratitude with others.

Shanti was a new and instant friend to whom I felt warmly drawn. Her kind heart shone through her personality like sunshine streaming through clouds. As we got to know one another, we shared some of our life challenges as well as our personal breakthroughs. Within the first month of our budding friendship, I asked her if we could commit to bringing out the best in each other. She was thrilled with this invitation for us both to enhance a positive state of mind. Our commitment to connect in gratitude and to celebrate each other's good news became primary. From this base, we rejoice in each other's successes. We encourage each other when we fall. We listen compassionately, without judging when times are hard. We invite each other to find gifts in the pain. We jump for joy when one of us meets a goal. We inspire each other!

Gratitude in Business

Do you want to be successful in business? Practice gratitude with your customers, vendors, partners, and promoters. You've seen the plaques, "Thank you for your business," and "We appreciate your referrals."

What an impression it left on me when a colleague sent me a $50 gift card for referring a client her way. Another time, when I volunteered my time on a webinar for a friend, she surprised me with a beautiful bouquet of flowers the very next day. And one of my favorites was when my massage therapist said, "No charge today. You referred a new client my way, and I want to say thank you." Loyalty programs such as a free coffee after ten cups, or frequent flyer miles towards a free flight, represent a form of appreciation for customers, and they lead to customer retention.

So how might you be more generous in appreciating customers, vendors, or collaborators in business? How might you appreciate employees and service providers?

Thank You, Everything

To feel grateful when times are good is easy. To appreciate others for their kindness is a delight. To feel grateful in the midst of disappointment, loss, or unjust accusations is a noble task. Michael Singer, the author of *The Untethered Soul: The Journey Beyond Yourself*, explained his attitude of gratitude during an interview with Oprah on Super Soul Sunday.

When Oprah asked Singer about the six-year lawsuit against his software company, Singer responded, "From the moment that took place, peace came over me, and I just rested back into it; and my attitude was, 'My God, this is a once in a lifetime opportunity to let go of anything that is left of me.'...There was a part of me that...would never want to be in that situation. I didn't do anything [wrong]."

He went on to explain that he felt the situation was God's grace, as if God was reaching down to pull out whatever was left of his ego. Singer explained that he was grateful to be refined by God. He demonstrated the power of saying "Thank You" when times are hard.

Your soul is grateful to be on Earth learning lessons, purifying karma, clearing interference, and experiencing new activities. It appreciates the chance to love and be loved and to feel connected to all that is. The soul knows it is playing a part through its personality in a dualistic planet, Earth. According to the soul, just being here right now is reason to celebrate and be thankful.

Helen Keller said it well: "So much has been given to me; I have no time to ponder over that which has been denied." We all have the capacity to feel gratitude, independent of what is happening. Are you willing to choose gratitude for the lessons you are learning and the gifts you are bound to receive? Are you ready to give thanks for the obstacles that you must overcome? Can you adopt gratitude as an attitude?

As a student of life, experiment. See how your life transforms when you practice gratitude.

Welcome to Gratitude

Choose Gratitude. When gratitude is a state of being, you open to sustainable peace and appreciation of what is right here, right now.

Gems for the Journey

- The Sixth Wisdom is Choose Gratitude. The action is to appreciate everything. Inevitably, your mood lifts as you see and appreciate all the good things that you have in your life right now.
- A practice of gratitude is the simplest and fastest way to live a happier, more spiritual life, and to create more loving relationships. When you focus your attention on what is going right, you begin to see more of what is right. There is great power in expressing gratitude especially when life seems challenging.
- Expressing gratitude to another person can change not only your day, but their day too. It's an incredible gift that does not cost anything. Give appreciation to the ones you love.

Walking with the Wisdoms

- To prime your mind, start your day with gratitude. List as many items as possible that come to mind when you ask the question, "What am I grateful for?" Let new answers arise each time you do this exercise.
- When you have a difficult day, read over past gratitude lists and watch your mood lift. Remind yourself that your difficulties are messengers of transformation, shaping you into a better person. Say, "Thank you for the lessons I am learning."
- Make the commitment to give three appreciations a day. These can be to your beloved, children, friends, co-workers, even strangers. Appreciate others in creative and specific ways.
- Download the "Two-Minute Gratitude Activation" at: *www.ASoulInspiredLife.com/wisdoms*

Inner-Views for Journaling and Conversations

These are sentence stems that you are encouraged to complete and elaborate on. Take your time and see where your writing goes or how a conversation unfolds.

- I am grateful for . . .
- When I am grateful, I feel . . .
- The last authentic compliment I received was . . .
- To be thankful for the challenges in my life is. . .
- I can choose gratitude by . . .
- My gratitude prayer is . . .
- The person I am most grateful for today is . . . and here is why . . .

Pause and Remember:

- Life Is for You
- You Deserve Love
- Life Is Guiding You
- Take Inspired Action
- Learn as You Live
- Choose Gratitude

Wealth of Life

Simplicity fosters
enough to go around
for everyone.

In a mansion or a shack,
lack and wanting are poverty.
Gratitude is wealth of life.

Some have more,
Some have less,
More or less of what?

Toys or Time?
Possessions or Peace?
Luxury or Love?

It is when we find wealth in love,
that we
treasure people,
appreciate experience,
invest in the heart.

Gratitude is wealth of life.

WISDOM

Your Purpose Is to Give

"Everybody can be great because everybody can serve."

—MARTIN LUTHER KING, JR.
Baptist Minister and Civil Rights Activist

Wisdom Seven marks a capstone maturity on the path to a soul inspired life. It's as though you have arrived at the top of a mountain where there is a grand vista. You see that life is good. Your self-worth is healthy. You trust your intuition and courageously act in the world. You are a student of life. You feel gratitude. While celebrating all your newly found understanding brings exuberance, it is not enough. You have so much joy and zest for life that you want to share it! You crave to give back. And there are so many causes that need peaceful soldiers. The more Wisdom Warriors there are in the world, the better, and now you are one of them. The call to serve summons you.

Now is the time to express your inspiration for the good of all. Like Joseph Campbell's mythological hero, it is time to bring back the boon of your Wisdom journey to others. "The ultimate aim of the quest must be neither release nor ecstasy for oneself but the wisdom and power to serve others," Campbell said of the hero's journey. And so, the action that Wisdom Seven proposes is generous, selfless contribution. Your purpose is to give.

While Wisdom One reassures you with, "Life is for me," Wisdom Seven urges you to exclaim, "I am here for life!"

"While Wisdom One reassures you with, 'Life is for me,' Wisdom Seven urges you to exclaim, `I am here for life!'"

As you triumph through challenges and find more compassion within, you naturally choose to give back as the highest expression of inspiration. Self-importance grows old. Self-gratification is less enticing. Accumulating things loses its appeal. Giving becomes the expression of your soul, and you do it without a need to receive in return.

Wherever you are right now, you can find a way to give. You do not need to write a mission statement or sign a life-purpose agreement. Living a life of purpose comes naturally as an extension of your heart. You are already doing it.

When you use your talents and personality for the good, you contribute with your heart in your current situation. Watch how guidance shows up and life prompts you. It *will* prompt you, and your purpose will draw you towards it.

Once you live on purpose, your purpose will grow. You bloom where you are planted. Nothing drastic needs to change. You can let your calling show up one step at a time. Do your best right now with what is in front of you. Purpose is gradual and continual. More opportunities will present themselves. Primatologist, anthropologist, and animal activist, Jane Goodall, said, "Every individual matters. Every individual has a role to play. Every individual makes a difference What you do makes a difference, and you have to decide what kind of difference you want to make."

Attributes of Wisdom Seven – Your Purpose Is to Give:

- Generous
- Giving
- Kind
- Altruistic
- Compassionate
- Purposeful

As you practice inner-honoring, you are poised and anchored to share your purpose. If you are listening to your guidance, inspired in your actions, and courageously experiencing the splendors of planet Earth, you are treating your soul to a joy ride. If you are learning lessons while developing and purifying your character, you radiate a charismatic glow. If you are authentically grateful for your life circumstances, your friends, and your resources, you are in sync with your soul. If you give back in the ways that appear to you in each and every precious moment, your soul is singing an original song—your song! Sing on. The music of your soul becomes an offering to the world.

Walking for Water

In the spirit of Wisdom Seven – Your Purpose Is to Give, I want to share an inspiring story of four young American women who answered a collective call to serve. In my work with a nonprofit organization called "Save the Rain," I was honored to help these high school girls initiate a fund-raising project to change the lives of an entire village in Africa. Their goal was to provide clean water to the Tanzanian village of Makiba. At the Makiba primary school, there were more than 1,000 students who forfeited a great deal of their schooling to walk up to six hours a day for dirty water. The most promising, long-term solution was to install rainwater catchment systems. The young American women understood this and went about finding a way to bring those catchment systems to Makiba.

Why would four teenagers extend so much effort and relinquish personal play time to help families across the globe? They were inspired.

The girls first met each other on a service trip with "Rustic Pathways," a student program that combines travel, education, and philanthropy. Coming from Boston, West Palm Beach, San Diego, and Chicago, they arrived in Tanzania, Africa, with a desire for adventure, a commitment to environmental restoration, and a yearning to give to a country and people in need.

During their trip, they experienced village life. In many parts of Africa, women and children (especially girls) spend hours each day walking to rivers and streams to collect water and bring it back to their homes, schools, and communities. One day, the U.S. volunteers were asked to join the local students in "kuchota maji," fetching water.

During school hours, the group took off on a long and taxing walk. They collected five-gallon buckets of unclean water, weighing forty pounds each, and carried them back to the village. This journey was necessary for the survival of the community but may have also brought illness right to their door. Waterborne illness is a leading cause of death in Sub-Saharan Africa.

When the four high school students returned to America, they reached out to "Save the Rain" to raise funds for the rainwater catchment systems. Today, they are well on their way to funding the project by organizing fund-raising walks and runs in their respective cities. Also, more students across the country are joining the cause. You can learn about this campaign by looking up *SavetheRain.org/miles-for-maji,* where students continue to advocate for solutions to the global water crisis.

The Peace Tour

Working with these girls brought back memories of my own high school adventure, "The Peace Tour," where I first felt the pull of humanitarian service. I was at an impressionable age, and the tour changed my life and my world view.

It was 1986, the tail end of the Cold War, and our destination was the Soviet Union. The group's intention was to build bridges of connection through the youth of our two politically opposed countries. About 20 students from across the United States journeyed together in hope and in the name of peace.

Naively, I thought that our trip would surely make a profound difference. I left ready to be a catalyst for peace. Although peace did not prevail on any grand political scale, my internal commitment to peace did. "The Peace Tour" opened my eyes; but not in the ways I had dreamed nor in ways I was prepared to see.

The Russian government sheltered our delegation and screened us from experiencing "real life" in the cities of Leningrad, Moscow, and Kiev. The government-appointed "Intourist" travel guide showed us only the most prosperous parts of each city. We stayed in the best hotels, visited the exclusive schools and restaurants designed for the upper class, and met only the privileged students, the children of high-ranking political officials. We did not see the poverty and scarcity, the piles of coal on the streets, the drab and barren grocery centers, or the long lines for everyday essentials. We were not shown the tall, plain, and dreary cement apartment buildings. Instead, the Russian government had laid out a fantasy trip for us.

We saw through their facade. As an empath, I felt unease in the hypocrisy and was furious with the parade of fine museums, fancy meals, and flamboyant decor. Midway through the trip, my aggravation festered into a fever, chills, and fatigue. Too tired to keep up with the touring agenda, I chose one day to stay behind in the hotel to nurse my sore throat and aching body. The bus left for another museum, fine-dining experience, and carefully chosen sight-seeing excursion.

Even with a raw throat and brewing fever, my need to know more of the real conditions in Russia drove me out of the comfort of the international hotel and into the streets to observe everyday life. The further I strayed, the more I saw the colorless, austere, and depressing surroundings. Bundled in a warm scarf to keep my chill at bay, I walked through a gloomy, old part of the city, making shy eye contact with solemn, somber-faced people, most of whom were wearing black and grey. I sensed an overall vibe of repression. Of course, a lot has changed in the 30 years since. The Russia of today is not the U.S.S.R. of 1986.

I returned to the United States, stunned, sad, and sick with strep throat and on my way to scarlet fever. With a raw, red, and swollen throat, I could not even speak for five days. It was as if my body were mirroring my state of mind. I was speechless and devastated by what I had seen and felt in the U.S.S.R. My body provided a break, so I would not have to explain what I had internalized, but not yet processed. It afforded me time to assimilate my disappointment and dismay. "The Peace Tour" marked the end of a certain kind of innocence. I found out for myself the darker side of controlling regimes. This "rite-of-passage" trip initiated my lifelong resolve to model and promote freedom, self-expression, and peace. I spent the last years of high school volunteering in service clubs, speaking about peace at churches, leading the newcomer's guide club at our school, and raising money and clothing for homeless youth. I was hooked on helping in any way I could. I stopped taking my free life for granted.

Giving Feels Great

The impact of my high school peace tour has stayed with me to this day. While I was the first to admit I was depressed when I returned home, I was also the first to take some action for change. I learned that a sure way to feel better—to feel great—is by giving to others. When you contribute, how does it make you feel? Are there causes you are passionate about today?

You can lend a helping hand and make a difference. We are in this together, waving the flag of soul inspired change for a better humanity, a world where all beings receive respect and opportunity.

I believe the world is ready for transformation. There are massive problems waiting for inspired solutions. There are causes to support, campaigns to lead, and activations in consciousness just waiting to happen. Be ready. You may be used by Spirit to deliver a message, start a revolution, or ignite a global conversation. I hope that excites you. It could be one simple act that gets reform going. Before you know it, there is momentum, and change is on its way. You might even be the last to know that you are initiating or leading a cause.

Uprisings are not always planned by those who start them. Many big disruptors were initiated by one person responding to an inspired thought and acting on it, like Mahatma Gandhi and Martin Luther King, Jr. If other people resonate with your vision, they will feel drawn to jump on board with you, and thus will begin a movement toward change. When your inclination to speak up for some cause resonates with a collective pain, the chances of more people joining your cause is heightened. You will be united into a new kind of army—a league of love.

As explored in Wisdom Four – Take Inspired Action, living boldly may challenge you; but to create, to give, and to receive are an honor here on Earth. The choices are many and yours to make, but the opportunity to actualize your generosity is a magnificent gift of life. When you make an impassioned choice to do something towards positive change, and it is coupled with a strong knowing from the start that it is for you to do, then you can persevere with grace and a Divine lift under your wings.

Affirmations of Wisdom Seven – Your Purpose Is to Give:

- I am here to serve.
- Giving is my joy.
- Life is for me and I am for Life.
- I contribute with my loving presence.
- I naturally find ways to give to others.
- My relationships are balanced in giving and receiving.

Getting Clues, Not the Whole Vision

Inspiration may propel you to give boldly, but it may not tell you everything at once. It may drip insights, like clues, that lead you onward until the next insight is revealed. You learned this with Wisdom Three–Life Is Guiding You. Not seeing the whole vision at once may be a blessing because knowing a little can be less intimidating than knowing your full destiny in one grand flash. If you knew what you were going to accomplish, you might question your ability to succeed. You might be daunted by the grand-scale change or impact and the role you are destined to play. Possibly, the you of today would get nervous seeing the you you are becoming. It is usually stressful to see yourself as a "giant of change" before you've grown into those big shoes that you will someday fill. You may see a potential future and respond, "Really? You want me to manage that? Do *what*?"

The gap between who you are and who you are becoming can intimidate you like a wide mountain crevasse scares a climber on her way to the summit. It is the same gap that you may feel when the vision of a project seems momentous compared to what you've done to date. However, you can do something to narrow the gap. Take one small step at a time. Focus on what's in front of you right now (not tomorrow or next year), be present to the phase of the journey that you are in now.

Be forewarned that the process of changing the world can be tedious. While you start with your idealistic high, you will probably wear many hats and often need to do the hard work of crunching numbers, studying technology, documenting systems, reporting to stakeholders, and accomplishing any number of other administrative tasks. This is when you want to call upon your soul inspired intentions and the deeper purpose of your goals to fuel your passion and muster the stamina to tend to that fire and to follow through.

You may be asking, "How can I do what is ahead of me? How can I make what is mine to do a reality?" The *how you do it* will become clear when you first focus on the *why you do it* and find the passions that speak to you.

Discovering passion is foremost. Later, you can figure out how to accomplish that mission. When you find your pet peeves, you'll likely find your passion. What gets you up in the morning? What makes you tick? What tugs at your heart when you hear the news or encounter a person down on his or her luck?

One story or one conversation can set you on a course that will give a whole new purpose and meaning to your life. There are many examples of this in the world. When two friends heard about the need for socks in homeless shelters in a television news story, they decided to start a sock company called Bombas. For every pair of socks they sell, one pair goes to a homeless shelter. More than a million have been distributed.

Physician and anthropologist, Paul Farmer, was determined to help the people of Haiti fight tuberculosis and made it his life mission to provide medical assistance to the needy in Haiti and around the world. Many ordinary individuals serve in "AmeriCorps" helping in communities across the country. The options for service are countless.

If you aren't sure how you want to serve, you can begin by finding what is missing or needed in your immediate world, your backyard, and look for solutions. Ask, "What is wanted of me?" When you become aware of what is needed, you will be eager to give with caring and compassion. The ways in which you choose to give will be unique to you, in the way you can make the most of your talents and passions. But whatever your chosen service, I am certain that you will encounter a fabulous feeling of fulfillment in giving back.

When you know what inspires you, and you feel compelled, even if you have some trepidation, do it anyway, and do it well! The courage of taking inspired action will buoy you up. Don't hold back. Inspiration will lead you in the right direction.

Sylvia Somerville, *Inspired's* editor, wrote this haiku, which speaks to the support you can expect from the Benevolent Universe even if you feel shy or hesitant. Grace is always there as a loving presence:

> *Invisible winds*
> *move us forward even when*
> *we are not ready.*

With a strongly defined mission, the "how to" mechanics fall into place. People show up. You take classes, do research, learn from others, make mistakes, and stay in momentum. There is room for everyone who has the same mission. With allies, you can collaborate and support causes together with greater strength, and often with less effort.

In her book, *E Squared,* Pam Grout wonders what would happen "if the seven million readers of *Ladies Home Journal* [wondered] . . . *How could I make the world more loving?* The big problems we are so afraid of would be solved in a year. Seven million people concentrating on issues like that are an unstoppable force!"

The world witnessed the strength of group action on January 21, 2017, when the "Women's March," which began in the United States, became a worldwide protest of millions who advocated for human rights, safety, healthcare, and families. The March initiated a stronger spirit of activism in many of those involved.

A Chinese proverb based on an extract from *The Great Learning,* a first-century BC Chinese philosophical text, illuminates the natural advancement of generosity. It starts with light in the soul and extends to peace in the world.

If there is light in the soul,
There will be beauty in the person.
If there is beauty in the person,
There will be harmony in the house.
If there is harmony in the house,
There will be order in the nation.
If there is order in the nation,
There will be peace in the world.

Overcoming Obstacles

When you discover your missions or life purposes, the little and big ones, they will propel your forward, and you will rise to the occasion. But there may be the interference of inner obstacles to overcome. At the top of the list are often self-doubt, attachment to pleasing others, and pride. There will also be outer obstacles—financial, relationship, and technological challenges, as well as resource issues and possible opposition. Let's look at the inner obstacles first, because these are the ones that can talk you out of your life purpose.

If you do not overcome your need to please others, the world loses, and so do you. Take a stand and risk the disapproval of others. Do this, and you will be living in integrity with your soul.

Are you ready to stop listening to your limiting beliefs and the interference between your soul and personality? There is no seat at your philanthropic strategy table for fear. Your work, if you choose to accept it, is to challenge the false fears and take inspired action.

Common inner obstacles might be:
- fears of failure (or fears of success)
- angst about disappointing others

- false notions that you are not good enough
- comparing yourself to others
- rigid controlling of the outcome
- fears of rejection or disapproval

When you overcome these inner blocks, you are unstoppable! You know what else? You graciously become humble. I'm not talking about being insecure or having low self-worth—*not at all!* Lack of confidence is a symptom of a fear. Just like arrogance, insecurity is a sign of fear. I am referring to the humbleness of being a grand conduit. It takes releasing fear to allow inspired service to flow through you. In his book, *Letting Go*, Dr. David Hawkins writes, "The truly humble cannot be humbled. They are immune to humiliation. They have nothing to defend."

When you drop your angst, your defenses, (and sometimes aggressiveness), you'll get to work, giving. Providence will step in and help you out.

"If you do not overcome your need to please others, the world loses, and so do you."

Once you overcome inner obstacles, the outer challenges of technology, tactics, people, resources, finances, and so on, all become manageable. It may take tenacity, but your drive to accomplish a vision will support you in finding solutions. Also, now you know from Wisdom Three how to listen to your inner-and-outer guidance to make choices and receive grace.

Unpretentious Giving

If we are instruments of love, then we are here to improve the lives of the Earth, humanity, and all other living beings. As Yogi Bhajan, who brought kundalini yoga to the West, said, "You are here to serve, here to lift, here to grace, here to give hope and action, to give the very deep love of your soul to all those who are in need." The unpretentious and inspired do not need credit for their work. According to Yogi Bhajan, by giving from the heart without thinking of the result, you reconnect to Source, elevating your soul and fulfilling your destiny. This is a mark of true leadership.

My teacher David is a living example of selfless giving. His transmission of light penetrates. His luminous presence exudes empathy and compassion. Yet, he remains unknown to most of the world at large at his own choosing.

I once asked him why he did not attract larger crowds. He replied, "As the purpose of my life, to be a spiritual guide, became evident, I prayed to God to keep my life simple. I consented to my destiny as a spiritual teacher, as long as I could teach only small groups."

David taught formally for more than thirty-five years, drawing groups of a hundred or fewer. He attracted and nurtured a stable following without promoting himself. Communities formed organically around him. He wanted it that way. He said, "If the organization got bigger, it would be susceptible to corruption, politics, and more confusion. Simple is good. It is what I agreed to."

The process of renouncing pride and no longer identifying with your accomplishments may take time. But the autonomy and satisfaction that selfless service provides will be worth the effort. When you catch yourself taking credit for what you do, notice and then quietly step back. When you are feeling pumped up because people have complimented you, receive the kind words and then silently say to the Universe, "Thank you for allowing me to share my gifts." Challenge yourself to stop seeking credit.

If credit comes, so be it. Receive it in the spirit of reciprocity. Take in the appreciation for the sake of the one offering it. By receiving graciously, you give the giver joy and complete the cycle of appreciation. You also strengthen neuropathways of happiness.

While the personality may like the accolades, your soul values the giving: the passing along of good feelings, expressing love in action, and uplifting others.

When you choose to give without the need for credit, you may not know the ripple effect that you created. But you can trust that your love has had a domino effect. Imagine, the contagious smile you offered someone is now circulating the globe. Your random acts of kindness are catalyzing more of the same. Your sound advice to another is now being offered to a stranger at a crossroads in life. Maybe your simple exchange of humor became a line in a romantic comedy, or your invention of a new game with the neighbor's children is becoming a favorite pastime at the local playground. Yes, your love and giving are the legacy you bring to life, and, even if they go seemingly unnoticed or unrecorded, rejoice that they continue to circulate to those in need and are noted by the Universe.

"Your love and giving are the legacy you bring to life."

David shared a story how inspiration guided him to contribute to someone else's welfare. Driving to one of his classes in the slow lane, he had the thought, "Driving in the slow lane is a great metaphor for yielding to others and being aware of others' comings and goings." It was a random thought, but he decided to include it in that evening's presentation. Midway through the class, David said, "So, drive in the slow lane." But, as he recalls, the phrase came out awkwardly, and the point didn't seem so profound. He berated himself for such a clumsy inclusion.

The next week, one of the students eagerly approached David and told him: "Remember last week when you told us to drive in the slow lane. Well, I usually drive fast and avoid the slow lane, but I decided to take your advice. On the way home, I had a blowout. Because I was in the slow lane, I was able to quickly pull to the side and avoid any accident." David then understood how Providence had guided him to help.

The Gift of Empathy

Another way to give is through empathy. Building rapport and understanding is a commonplace method in sales, and in building good relationships. Rapport comes from understanding each other's ideas and feelings and communicating from that place. Empathy is a starting place for negotiation or reconciliation and perhaps mutual transformation. The following fable illustrates how empathy may require extreme measures.

> There was once a prince who would not join the royal table at meals. Instead, he sat under the table, imitating a chicken for he was sure he was one.
> The King and Queen called in a wise sage for help. The sage assessed the situation. Then she got down on the floor and joined the prince in his pecking and clucking. For some time, this satisfied them both. Eventually, the sage asked the Prince Chicken, 'I wonder what it is like at the table. Do you think the food is any better?'

They discussed the possibility for a while, and then the two chickens decided to sit at the royal table to eat the feast. Over time, with companionship, the prince became a prince again.

This fable illustrates how important it is to use inspired empathy to uplift others. Even if you think you look silly or feel strange about what you are prompted to do or say, sometimes these very actions can rescue someone or turn a situation around and become a way to give to the world.

My friends, Bill and Joann Truby, cofounders of "Truby Achievements," call this being "other-centered." They teach that an other-centered approach is primarily about awareness. Bill states, "When you can see, and even understand, the reason for another person's words, attitude, and behavior, you are in the best space possible to interact, serve, or even protect yourself. From words, to love languages, to personality styles, the most meaningful impact comes from positioning all that you say and do in the style of the other person. In fact, that is THE way to connect."

What the World Needs

"I never perfected an invention that I did not think about in terms of the service it might give others. I find out what the world needs, then I proceed to invent." This quote is attributed to Thomas Edison. If you are in business, a giving intent is to find solutions to problems—whether your work is for profit, nonprofit, or pro bono.

As a fan of conscious capitalism and social entrepreneurship, I see business as an arena to uplift humanity and make the world a better place.

I spent my thirties earning an income while in service to the Amazon rainforest. Working with Amazon John Easterling, we sold rainforest botanicals in the United States, Canada, and Europe. The enterprise turned out to be profitable, but that was not my drive. I was passionate about rainforest preservation and health.

The Amazon Herb Company had its roots in the vision of Nicole Maxwell. She believed that the healing properties of rainforest botanicals offered prevention and support for some of the leading causes of death in the Western world.

Nicole first ventured into the Amazon on behalf of pharmaceutical companies to explore the drug potential of rainforest plants and their chemical components. She soon discovered, thanks to the rainforest shamans, that whole plant medicines do not pose negative side effects like patented drugs do. Pharmaceuticals only mimic part of the plant wisdom— not the full array of complementary biochemistry found in the plant's natural form. In whole-plant medicine, the herb's chemicals are balanced and yield synergistic effects.

Harvesting botanicals is an honorable livelihood for indigenous people, unlike excessive logging and clear cutting. Fair compensation allows them to cancel logging contracts and gain title to thousands of acres of rainforest. This was, and continues to be, one of the many profound impacts of our work in the jungle.

Promoting rainforest botanicals creates a better future for our planet, as the rainforests are the lungs that contribute greatly to oxygenating Earth, insuring an environmental balance.

Losing the rainforests means not only a loss of quality of life for the globe but also a loss of the potent healing plants.

Through a series of events, Nicole Maxwell and John Easterling met. With her invitation, John carried forth her vision and made it his mission. John's near-death experience in the jungle and a powerful healing with its indigenous herbs taught him the power of the rainforest. A treasure hunter by trade, John switched direction with the epiphany, "All these years I'd been in search of lost treasures, when in truth, the real treasure of the rainforest is the rainforest itself, her healing botanicals."

To bring his new mission to life, Amazon John looked for a sales team, which he called ambassadors. I jumped on board in the company's early years. My focus quickly became education. I taught people the power of healing through South American herbs, and I simultaneously exposed them to a way to help save the rainforest from rapid deforestation. For the next ten years, health education became my passion, and in the process, I recruited and led a sales team. Through these efforts, I found both fulfillment and abundance. I became a business leader, trainer, spokesperson, and advisor without intending to do so, but rather by doing what lay in front of me.

Using Financial Resources to Serve

With the financial flow that working with the Amazon Herb Company offered me, I chose to be a steward of money, in accordance with my values. By contributing to causes you believe in, you change the world. The power of money that is used for the good of humanity is a power that propels peace. Indeed, you vote with your dollars. How will you vote today?

When you do good with the resources bestowed upon you, you are circulating money to create positive change.

John Easterling teaches that there are three reasons to have money:

1. to reach your highest potential
2. to support the ones you love
3. to give to the causes you believe in

Lynne Twist, philanthropist, educator, and author of *The Soul of Money*, writes, "*The Soul of Money* offers a way to realign our relationship with money to be more truthful, free, and potent, enabling us to live a life of integrity and full self-expression that is consistent with our deepest core values, no matter what our financial circumstances." Her invitation is to "embrace its flow." She believes we can engage in the economy in ways that are healing and sustainable, and support the thriving and blessing of all involved.

No matter how much money you have in the bank or in your wallet, tithing and donating sends an abundance signal that keeps the flow of money circulating in your life. Rejoice that you are able to give, whatever the amount. Visualize your offering multiplying. As you demonstrate generous stewardship, you open yourself to the currency of prosperity.

I celebrate the growing number of companies that originate for a social purpose and/or donate to humanitarian and environmental causes. Eileen Fisher, a women's clothing brand, utilizes nonconventional models—sometimes employees—to showcase simple beauty in all its forms. With the founder Eileen Fisher at the helm, the company initiates and maintains many programs to empower women, including the Eileen Fisher Leadership Institute. On its website, the company states, "Envision a new future filled with possibilities for personal and social empowerment—a future rooted in bravery, self-compassion and listening to our bodies."

4Ocean is a company that removes trash from oceans and coastlines around the world, twenty-four hours a day, seven days a week. It started in 2017 when two surfers went on a vacation to Bali and were devastated by the amount of plastic they saw in the ocean. So they decided to do something about it. They created a company, which is flourishing: Less than two years later, 4Ocean employs 150 people worldwide and has removed nearly two million pounds of plastic debris. How do they fund their operation? They are selling bracelets (and other products) from 100 percent recycled plastic for $25 each. According to the website *4Ocean.com*, "By giving ocean plastic a value, we are creating a new economy for the removal of trash."

Turning the Tides Towards Positivity

Just as acts of service change the world, so do uplifting shifts of consciousness. As exhibited throughout *Inspired*, an inner transformation often precedes the outward expression. Once we awaken to the realization that we are all interconnected, we change: We become less judgmental. We give up fighting against the wrongs of the world and focus on solutions. We give up the fighting inside of our own minds, too.

War has become an overused metaphor in the world of activism: "The war on drugs. The war on violence. The fight against cancer. The fight against terrorism. The anti-poverty program, and so on . . . " This creates an atmosphere of opposition, instead of union. Mother Theresa knew this and once said, "I will never attend an anti-war rally; if you have a peace rally, invite me." When you are *for* something, you give power to the current of positive change. And the tides can turn when enough of us move toward positivity.

To be a contributor to this positive change, find within yourself some energizing gratitude. This will move you into a place of peace. Your energy affects everyone. Simply being at ease, emanating happiness, and feeling gratitude sends a signal that reverberates in the far reaches of the universe—and it may lead to concrete results in your neighborhood, too.

There have been many experiments that have demonstrated how energy can create peace. In 1993, one carefully controlled scientific study showed that several hundred people practicing transcendental meditation over a three-week period brought the violent crime rate down in Washington, DC, by more than twenty percent. I believe we can reduce conflict and promote harmony in our work and home environments through maintaining a peaceful presence. When Wisdom Warrior, Panache Desai, was asked how to approach work, he said, "Our job is the excuse through which we get to love people. We are put in exactly the place that we need to be to love the people that we are around."

Your energy contributes to the collective. Your integrity, humor, and caring are broadcast on the energy air waves that unite us all, and especially those in close physical proximity or those who are on your mind. Yes, distance prayer for a person or a purpose has also been studied, and the results are in: Remote healing works. And you don't need any credentials or training to do it. You simply need passion, heart, and a concentrated focus on love.

Giving in Relationships

One of the most obvious places to give is in your relationships—in your circle of family, co-workers, and friends. When those in your inner circle need support, offer deep, empathetic listening—loving awareness, not a predetermined "fix-it" mentality. As a listener, rest in a compassionate space and observe from a higher perspective. Acknowledge that the other person has an inner teacher who is there to guide them.

You can reflect back what you hear. You might start with a statement of validation that shows you "get it." Something like, "Wow, I hear that you feel _____." (fill in the blank). Next repeat what you heard, and then you might ask, "Did I hear you correctly? Did I miss anything? Is there more you would like to share?" Give the other time to express, be heard, and process.

Then you might ask, "Do you want help seeing the situation from a higher perspective?" Or, "Do you need to talk? How can I best serve you right now?" This is so empowering to others. They will feel that you have confidence in them, which builds their confidence. Offer perspective if they request it. Otherwise, ask them empowering questions like, "What are your options? What do you think you could do right now to feel better? How might you get through this?" You get the idea. You become a facilitator of their inner knowing, propelling them towards inner-honoring. If there are ongoing issues or patterns, you may find an appropriate time to shed light on their shadow or encourage them to find professional help.

When giving to others, be sure you feel drawn to help. Are you comfortable being there? Be mindful not to over-give and build resentment. It is extremely important to monitor your energy for the long haul. Be careful not to care-take at the expense of your own health and resources. Care-taking is a disservice to your relationships. It can enable another to feel disempowered, incapable, or weak. Instead, empower your friends.

In our society, quite often, "friendship" means helping friends feel good, no matter what. It's being unequivocally on their side, even if that means agreeing with their sense of victimhood. This is a slippery slope. Soul inspired friends are honest, and they help each other see blind spots—like what they have been hiding inside and hiding behind.

This is an awakened relationship sustained by honesty, sincerity, and healing. Trust me, it is the fast track to spiritual growth. It does, however, take both people to establish this kind of soul inspired connection. It might be a shift from keeping things "copcetic and groovy." But the more dedicated you and your loved ones are to evolution, the more you'll propel each other. You commit to offering wise, alternative perspectives. With an honoring tone, and with permission, you'll find this kind of loving interaction extremely rewarding, especially if you are aiming to be a Wisdom Warrior. Believe me, you want insightful friends that call you out and question you when you are living a lie, acting out of fear, falling into victimhood, or missing the mark.

With synergy, soul inspired friends increase the grace in each other's life.

A Life of Giving

If the intentions of your actions are soulful, concerned with expressing your purpose, there is no regret. When you come from a spirit of giving, you will feel good about yourself and what you've accomplished. It is not yours to judge if you gave in big or small ways. All giving is good giving. Indeed, a life of love, play, and service is a life well-lived.

Welcome to Giving
Your Purpose is to Give. Giving is a natural outpouring of your joy. It propels your purpose, and a life of service is a whole lot more fun, too.

Gems for the Journey

- The Seventh Wisdom is: Your Purpose Is to Give. The action is selfless contribution. As you live the soul inspired way, you find more contentment within, and you naturally choose to give back as the highest expression of inspiration.
- Money is a means to contribute to causes you believe in. You can align your spending and your vocation with solutions for a better world.
- Your love and the energy you bring to life are your legacy. You can give to the world in each moment with your intention and kindness. You can give to friends with compassionate listening and honest perspective.

Walking with the Wisdoms

- What causes are you passionate about? Make a list. Next, ask yourself, "How can I give more to these causes?" Choose a nonprofit organization and donate to it. You can give time, expertise, your influence, or money. Look at your life and consider if you can contribute regularly. In what ways? How much? How often?
- Practice the affirmation: "I am here to serve." As you move through your day and interact with people, be aware of how you might be more caring, a better listener, or how you might offer your assistance.
- Connect with a friend or family member and discuss how your relationship could improve. How might

you be more honest with each other? How might you encourage each other to live from love, not fear?
- Download the "Two-Minute Generosity Activation" at: *www.ASoulInspiredLife.com/wisdoms*

Inner-Views for Journaling and Conversations

These are sentence stems that you are encouraged to complete and elaborate on. Take your time and see where your writing goes or how a conversation unfolds.

- My purpose is . . .
- Giving is . . .
- The ways I like to give are . . .
- I am generous when . . .
- Areas of my life where I most need credit are . . .
- The friendships I want to improve include . . .
- To be humble means . . .

Pause and Remember:

- Life Is for You
- You Deserve Love
- Life Is Guiding You
- Take Inspired Action
- Learn as You Live
- Choose Gratitude
- Your Purpose Is to Give

Give to Life

How can I give to life?
How can I live and be true?
How can I live in love?
That's all I want to do!

I see it in the trees blowing in the winds
they're blowing
I see it in the sun bowing at sunset.

I see it in the flowers blooming in the spring
they're blooming
I see it in the ocean tide rolling in.

Just remember who I am,
Remember.
Just surrender to the now,
And "what is" will show me how . . .

CONCLUSION

Living a Soul Inspired Life

"Inspiration without action is merely entertainment."

—MARY MORRISSEY

Life Coach, Motivational Speaker, and Founder of
Life Mastery Institute

As we come to the end of *Inspired*, I hope you are steady on your journey of living a soul inspired life. Continue to practice the Wisdoms. Continue learning. Most importantly, go out and really live. Give it your all. Joyously and courageously, raise the bar on your life. It is application time. Ready or not, here we go. You've got this.

The Notes of Your Life

The Seven Wisdoms are here to escort you into your soul inspired life. In the Introduction, I described the Seven Wisdoms as notes on a scale. Each Wisdom resonates to a different tone, but together, they create infinite melodies and a multitude of harmonies. Now that you are familiar with the Wisdoms, compose your own songs. Sing the notes in any order and in various combinations to create the song called your life! Let's review the Wisdom notes.

Wisdom 1 – Life Is for You: You *trust* and know that life is for you. The Universe is benevolent and has blessings to bestow upon you.

Wisdom 2 – You Deserve Love: With *inner-honoring*, you deeply feel that you deserve all the love and the good coming your way.

Wisdom 3 – Life Is Guiding You: By following inner-and-outer *guidance*, life prompts you to receive your good.

Wisdom 4 – Take Inspired Action: With the *courage* to move forward on these promptings, you take inspired action.

Wisdom 5 – Learn as You Live: You are *learning*, evolving, and becoming a better version of you.

Wisdom 6 – Choose Gratitude: You *appreciate* and are filled with gratitude for your life—even the hard stuff.

Wisdom 7 – Your Purpose Is to Give: With *generosity*, you are giving back and contributing to life.

Now your big wins arrive as you watch what unfolds from what you've learned. You've opened your heart, challenged beliefs, and shifted paradigms. You have watched your fears lessen, and your trust, self-worth, and confidence grow. I'm so excited for you because now you get to watch for changes in your life. Trust me, they will happen, and they are going to be positive. Expect transformation: It is a blessing that comes with this book.

You will view your life with a different lens—guaranteed. And with that shift in perspective, some surprise windfall could come your way, like a new relationship, a career opportunity, or unexpected adventures and invitations. Or, you may experience changes in more subtle ways, like an overall sense of grace, contentment, and healthy self-esteem. You may notice you react less defensively to triggers, that your brilliance is shining through your personality, and that you are making choices that are in line with your soul instead of fear. You may find that coincidences abound and that you are drawn to feeling grateful and to giving to others.

Show the world what you've got! Get happy and do *your* thing. The authentic you is the joyful you, and humanity can use a dose of joy right about now.

Yippee, It's Great to Be Me

When I was eight, I entered a T-shirt design contest. Our church organizers had picked out a playful image for the front of the shirts and invited the community's youth to suggest words to accompany it. The image was that of a gleeful squirrel floating in the air with a beautiful maple leaf as her sail. The squirrel's big grin seemed contagious. What came to me was a simple phrase, an expression of what I imagined the squirrel was thinking— "Yippee it's great to be me!"

I entered, and won the contest. I don't remember what I won (maybe a T-shirt). What I do remember is seeing all my church friends wearing this very affirmative message, and how happy it made us all feel.

Winning that contest preceded this book by four decades. I've been a champion of self-worth ever since. Like the squirrel T-Shirt, the message of *Inspired* is to fall in love with you. It's my honor to cheerlead you on in your inspired life. I'm raising my hands now and singing, "2,4,6,8, you can do this, you are great!" I imagine you expressing the authentic you and sharing in your inspiration. I envision you doing a good deed and singing your heart song.

Start Where You Are

LIFE is a process.

We are all in different places in our evolution and in the process of embodying the Seven Wisdoms. For some of you, the Wisdoms feel familiar. They may be more of a reminder of what you already know to be true, and what you practice. You resonate with their principles. For others, you are charting some new territory with the Wisdoms, exploring paradigm shifts and soul-centered philosophies that take time to assimilate. Take your time. Like training in high altitudes before attempting a summit, you must acclimate. Start where you are: Make these Wisdoms your own.

Working with the Seven Wisdoms is not a one-shot deal because life is more like a spiral than a straight line, a continual evolution of learning.

Expect that your personal growth themes will surface again and again. You will regularly encounter your greatest desires and your biggest fears. When you notice yourself returning to life lessons and themes, you might smile and say, "Here I am again!" But with each pass on the spiral, you will notice that you have changed since the last time. You will meet your life with greater clarity, a greater depth of consciousness.

At certain junctures in your life, one Wisdom or another will take precedence and serve as a messenger. By working with *Inspired*, you'll know which Wisdom you are passing through.

While the Wisdom you visit is the same one you encountered before, you are not the same: You see more of the principles. You understand more. Your perspective has changed. You apply the suggestions in ways that are relevant to a new day. So, move in-and-out of particular Wisdoms as you need them. You can call upon their power when life's events nudge you towards one lesson or another.

Remember, you do not need to *find* empowerment. It is what you already have. When you take full responsibility for your life, you feel a power within you. This genuine and reliable power propels you forward and makes things right for you and for the world. Most importantly, you like who you are becoming.

Inspiration Moment by Moment

The more you practice a life in-Spirit, the more you establish a caring, compassionate, and connected way of living. The path of inspiration is not supernormal, but the new normal. It is *how* you live, not what you *do,* that sustains a soul inspired life. In

other words, your intentions and the moment-by-moment journey—not the destination—matter most. The best of feelings—faith, joy, and happiness—become the reassurance that you are indeed on the path of a soul inspired life.

Inspiration can be found in simple moments—when you hold a newborn child, help a friend, prepare a wholesome meal, complete a project, pick up litter, or donate to a nonprofit organization. You might spontaneously let someone go ahead of you in line or do any random act of kindness. Inspiration works through all of us as we are doing simple things for the betterment of our world.

Everyday kindness changes lives—one life at a time. Behind the limelight we can all serve in extraordinary ways. So, decide what you want to nurture in this life. You gain self-respect when you stand in integrity with your soul, in integrity with love. You believe what you repetitively think, so think good thoughts.

My deepest wish is that you walk in happiness on your soul inspired path, that you enjoy the views along the way and share them with the ones you love.

I invite you to continue experimenting. In the Appendix you'll find more tools that accompany *Inspired*, including information about *The Inspired Guidebook*.

I encourage you to utilize these Seven Wisdoms as they were intended as gems for your journey. Put them in your pocket, and let's keep walking. In-joy!

APPENDIX

Inspired Glossary

Bright Genius – The brilliant inspiration that flows through you. A muse, a magical impulse, or a flash of dazzling imagination; it is the creative energy that uses you as a conduit for inspiration. A bright genius is behind the greatest works of art, humor, ingenuity, inventions, and thought leadership.

Choice Points – Pivotal moments when you are called to make a decision that alters the trajectory of your life. Because decisions have consequences, the future calibrates according to not only your decision but also the intention behind it. An opportunity to make a conscious decision.

Divine Order – A Higher Order and timing for the unfoldment of good. A universal system of benevolence for all concerned. Seen from a soul perspective, life unfolds in Divine Order.

Ego – A part of the personality that identifies itself as separate. It defends its identity by comparing itself to "other." A sense of self-importance or inferiority. The image you have of yourself.

Embody – To be an expression of or give a tangible or visible form to an idea, wisdom, quality, or feeling. To personify, manifest, symbolize, represent, incarnate, and exemplify.

Flow State – Being connected to the *now*, where a moment-to-moment ease mingles within activity. A state of being that trusts life, lets go of control, and invites inspiration to lead the way.

Holistic Learning – The acquisition of knowledge or skills through direct experience and study. Holistic learning is the process of speeding up your development by assimilating, and absorbing through your mental, physical, and emotional faculties.

Inspiration – Living in Spirit, to be filled with light. Receiving a positive impulse to do or feel something uplifting; to be stimulated to create good for your benefit and the benefit of others. Breathing in.

Interference – The negative beliefs, unconscious programming, toxins, emotions, or moods that get in the way of your personality aligning with your soul. Can also be negative influences that block you from feeling love.

Intuition – The natural ability to know or understand without reasoning. An inner knowing, wisdom, or gut feeling. Intuition expresses itself as your hunches, premonitions, sixth-sense, insights, or small inner voice.

Personal Transformation – A thorough or dramatic change, alteration, or metamorphosis of character, personality, and habits. The ability to take personal developmental experiences and apply them in life. A natural result of living a soul inspired life.

Personality – The combination of behavior, emotion, motivation, and thought patterns that define an individual. Includes your ego, character, talents, and skills. When your personality aligns with your soul, you utilize the personality for the greater good.

Shadow – The unconscious parts of you that you disown, reject, hide, and keep in the dark. If not recognized, the shadow can rule your life. When recognized, the shadow becomes a doorway to liberation.

Signs – Messages from the Universe offering you guidance. They appear as symbols, dreams, people, metaphors, coincidences, and random happenings that clearly give you a nudge towards an action or change. Signs can also be a confirmation.

Soul – The immortal you: that which you are before you are born and after you die. Pure energy and love. Part of Spirit, like a drop of the ocean. When you allow your soul to lead the way, your personality is utilized for the good, and you live a soul inspired life.

Soul Evolution – The soul's process of developing and expanding in consciousness. As you integrate your soul's evolution, you value love over things of the material world. You gain a growing sense of your connection to all that is.

Spirit – Loving energy that elicits awe and feels like bliss. While indescribable, it goes by many names, such as Creative

Intelligence, Unified Field, Source, the Divine, God, Oneness, the Universe, and Love.

Successing – A verb that celebrates success as a process, not a destination. The focus is on who you are becoming and the experience you are having while reaching for a goal.

Wisdom – A principle that gives you the ability to think and act using knowledge, experience, understanding, and insight. An essential intelligence for evolution. True wisdom arrives when you are humble.

Wisdom Warrior – A person who models a soul inspired life and teaches by example, guidance, and life lessons. (That's you!)

APPENDIX

Inner-Honoring Activities

Inner-honoring activities are concrete ways to care for yourself and create a more sustainable and soul inspired life.

There are three types of inner-honoring activities:
1. *Two-Minute Resets* – one an hour
2. *Twenty-Minute Turnarounds* – one a day
3. *Two-Hour Renewals* – one a week

Two-Minute Resets are extremely useful when you are ultra-busy and only have a moment to get refreshed. Ideally, you do one an hour. (They are treats to enjoy.)

Some examples of *Two-Minute Resets* are:
- Drinking water or another restorative beverage
- Stretching your body
- Shaking, jumping up and down, or jumping rope

- Listening to a favorite song or piece of instrumental music
- Taking a short walk around the block or up and down the stairs
- Tapping or using EFT (Emotional Freedom Technique)
- Writing down a list of things and people for whom you are grateful
- Listening to a prerecorded audio of your voice affirming positive statements
- Breathing deeply and consciously (such as breath of fire, equal breathing, alternative nostril breathing, and other breathing techniques)
- Petting or spending time with an animal
- Reading an inspirational passage
- Hugging a loved one (or a quick snuggle)
- Going outside and communing with nature
- Listening to one of the "Two-Minute Wisdom Activations"

After looking at the above list, consider what activities fill you up and last about two minutes. Create your own list of *Two-Minute Resets* that will boost your energy.

I recommend that you engage in one *Two-Minute Reset* every hour.

When it's time for a Reset, your pick will depend on what you have been previously doing. If you've been sitting and thinking, you may want to get up and move. If you've been physically active, you may want to slow down and breathe. You'll know what to do. This practice is a discipline that pays off and will build on itself.

Twenty-Minute Turnarounds are activities that take more time and space but result in a greater recharge.

Some examples of *Twenty-Minute Turnarounds* include:
- Engaging in a recreational activity or exercise (make sure you are doing what you love)
- Taking time in nature to connect and observe
- Doing a brief yoga session or stretching activities (add music)
- Getting a chair massage
- Soaking in a tub
- Writing in your journal
- Envisioning your bright future and setting intentions with creative visualization
- Reading a chapter of an uplifting book
- Listening to an inspiring podcast (while resting or walking)
- Meditating with a guided audio or following your breath
- Calling an encouraging friend (set the intention for your time, making sure the exchange is positive and supportive in nature)
- Re-centering your thinking. Assess your negative thoughts and turn them towards positive perspectives. (See the Appendix where I explain "Start Where You Are Affirmations.")

Design your list of *Twenty-Minute Turnarounds* and include any of the above suggestions that resonate for you. Get creative with this list. These personal demonstrations of love are for your pleasure. I invite you to enjoy at least one turnaround a day, and the best way to ensure you do this is to schedule your turnarounds as non-negotiable appointments with yourself.

Commit to a conscious date with you, a date to honor yourself and renew.

The brave and bold find time every week for **Two-Hour Renewals**. Pull out your calendar now. Can you find two hours every week or, at the minimum, every other week to treat yourself to a renewal? Renewals foster big shifts. Two-Hour Renewals have the power to restore you deeply from the inside out. When you respect these renewals as special times, you can transform yourself over time. Truly, renewals prevent burnout and overwhelm.

Here are some examples of *Two-Hour Renewals*:
- Enjoying an extended recreational activity like hiking, biking, or fishing
- Receiving a long massage or body-work treatment
- Experiencing a therapeutic session (counseling or coaching)
- Creating and/or reviewing your values, life goals, or purpose
- Making a treasure map of what you want in your life
- Playing in *The Inspired Guidebook*
- Spending quiet time in nature (taking photos, laying down and day dreaming, strolling)
- Attending a personal-development class
- Listening to a live or recorded concert that uplifts you
- Visiting a special place
- Driving on country roads
- Playing a musical instrument for the fun of it, in a flow state

- Having a personal spa day (at a spa or at home). How about a mani/pedi, plus a facial scrub and a tub. By the way guys—you would like this, too.

You can create and store your unique inner-honoring activities in a journal, on 3 x 5 cards, in your computer, or in the Notes section of your phone. Have the lists readily available so that every hour, every day, and every week you can choose and engage in your Resets, Turnarounds, and Renewals. Over time, these activites will become automatic. You'll add to the lists and find out what works best for you. The important thing is to *schedule the activities in your calendar*. Make this real for you!

APPENDIX

Start Where You Are
Affirmations

Start Where You Are Affirmations meet you where you are. Think about it, if you are practicing affirmations that do not feel true, what is the use in stating them? If you use affirmations that don't reflect what is real for you, no matter who designed them—including the *Seven Wisdoms* affirmations—you can do more harm than good. I suggest you alter them in order to grow and evolve into them. For example, you can say, "I am willing to learn how life is for me. I am willing to learn to love myself. I am willing to learn to be courageous," and so on.

Don't you think this is better than the incongruence of trying to say something you just don't believe yet? When you do not believe your statements, you will not be able to secure your mind's consent to create them. Instead, the effort may cause pain, distance, and turmoil.

You cannot talk yourself into change. You cannot say, "I am happy, My life is great, I love my body," when what you are thinking is "I'm sad, Life sucks, I'm fat." Inwardly, you might be hoping that merely parroting positive words could convince you otherwise, but the words are too far from the truth. Instead of feeling at ease, you feel conflicted. So, what do you think happens if you force words and thoughts that are way ahead of your growth? You pretty much feel what you hoped you would not. In this case, sad, disappointed, and fat—not to mention *frustrated*. The resistance persists. This does you harm, not good. According to author and Buddhist nun, Pema Chödrön, "Resistance to unwanted circumstances has the power to keep those circumstances alive and well for a very long time. When the resistance is gone, so are demons."

Where the negative self-talk was, "I'm sad, I'm fat," replace it with, "I am willing to learn to be happier." *Ah! Now that feels true.* Crafting statements that reflect where you are now is the starting place that results in embracing positive affirmations of your own: "I am willing to find some goodness in life, I am willing to love myself as I am."

Over time, the statements become an evolving continuum into better feeling affirmations. Once you've acknowledged and accepted what is taking place in your mind and life, you can find peace with it.

When you are at peace, you change. In time, you'll outgrow an affirmation and create a new one that fits. As you grow towards your desired state, you expand your affirmations to match. It's a little like buying new shoes when your feet are growing.

Create your Start Where You Are Affirmations with statements like:

I am willing to _____

I know I will learn to _____

I am willing to learn to _____

I am open to learning how to _____

I am moving towards _____
I'm on my way to believing_____

Fill in the blanks with where you want to go—your desired state, your goal, the bullseye of your inspired life. You will find that the results are amazing. Starting with where you are, you notice that over hours, days, or weeks, your affirmations get clearer. You are real with yourself, and that is when affirmations work! You become even more willing.

Below are some examples of 7 Wisdoms Start Where You Are Affirmations:

- I am willing to learn to trust life.
- I look forward to seeing the good in this situation.
- I'm on my way to believing that I am enough.
- I know I will learn to trust my intuition.
- I am willing to learn to be uncomfortable.
- I am open to learning to be my authentic self with others.
- I am learning to love to learn.
- I am moving towards a better attitude, where I am grateful.
- I am learning to see the gifts I can give and contribute to life.

Start where you are, not even one-step ahead. To falsify your evolution, if only to yourself, dis-graces the journey.

APPENDIX

Saying "No" with Poise, Clarity, and Respect

You can learn how to say no with poise, clarity, and respect. When you commit to inspired action, you will be moved to say no at times. You learn to say "no," with the bigger "yes" in mind. Below are six techniques. Remember, no guilt necessary.

Postpone Your "No." This is simple. If you aren't sure, or you don't feel confident enough to say "no" right away, you can instead postpone your "no." Here's how.

"Thanks for asking. I need to consult my _____ (family, calendar, team, or spouse—fill in the blank)."

Then ask when your response is required.

Assure the person that you will be in touch by then, and tell them how—by calling, texting, emailing, or sharing in person.

Get back to the person in the timeframe and manner you promised. You might include one of the following technniques for saying "no" gracefully if "no" is what you decide.

Sandwich Your "No." Include positive remarks before and after delivering the "no" message.

"Thank you for _____ [the opportunity, the compliment, thinking of me . . .] I really appreciate it (or appreciate you).

Right now, I am not able to _____ (repeat the request)."

Or simply say, "Right now I have to say 'no.'"

From here, you can conclude with a genuine compliment about the person, opportunity, organization. Perhaps you offer an alternative (see below), or express your gratitude.

Offer an Alternative to "No." This technique can be added to the sandwich or used as a stand-alone "no" response. The technique is simple. You might say, "I can't do that, but I can do this."

For example, "I can't sit on the board, but I could be an advisor."

"I can't coach the kid's soccer team, but I can commit to helping out with four practices this season." "I'm not available, but I could refer you to someone who may be interested."

I Have a "No" Policy. When you say you have a policy, others don't take your "no" personally. For example:

"We have a 'no smoking at our office' policy." Or, "I have a policy that I don't stay out after 9 pm on weeknights." You get the idea. Similarly, you might say, "This is not in my scope of work," or, "This is not in our business agreement."

Priority Swap "No." This response works with co-workers, supervisors, housemates, and family members. If someone asks you to take on more responsibility, you might remind that person that you can only do that if he or she can take something else off your to-do list. You might invite the asker to help discern your priorities with respect to your joint roles and projects.

"I can only take on (this new project) if I let go of (another responsibility). Which do you prefer I do?"

No Excuse "No." All too often, we think we need to explain our "no" responses, and we bore others with our long lists or reasons, overwhelm, and excuses. It is okay to say,

"Thank you, but I can't right now." or "No, my plate is full." Or simply, "I appreciate you asking, but I'm going to say 'no.'" In other words, just say "no" without the need to explain your reasons.

Saying "no" is honest, empowering, and it breaks care-taking patterns. Have no guilt. Get real. You cannot be everything to everyone. When you don't need to justify the "no" to yourself is when you don't need to justify it to others.

APPENDIX

Good Company Assessment Sheet

The influences in your life, predict the future of your life. Remember the story of my Mt. Shasta summit with the experienced climber, Laurie? Or the Indian Guru who counseled, "the way to enlightenment is good company?" Good company comes in the form of people, music, activities, books, and thoughts.

Make a list in each category of the main influences in your life.

Next assess: Does this person, media, activity, or thought give me energy or take energy? Rate from -5 to +5.

In the action box, give yourself better suggestions. How might you change or eliminate the influences that deplete you? How might you enhance the ones that uplift and energize you?

For example, you may see that listening to the news is draining you, and choose to watch TED Talks that energize you, instead. You might identify someone in your life that complains and brings you down. This gives you the choice to talk with them about it, and/or spend less time with them. Conversely, you may realize how much you enjoy another person and initiate more connection time. If something or someone uplifts you, do more of it.

As you go through the assessment process, take your time. Study your life, and notice the energy in your body when you are with people, media inputs, or even when you hear your own chronic thoughts. Ask yourself, "Does this give me energy or take it?"

Inventory of Your Influences	Rate -5 to 5+	Your Change Actions
People in Your Life		
Read, Listen, & Watch		
Free Time Activities		
Thoughts You Think		

APPENDIX

Inspired Resources

from favorite Wisdom Warriors
(Includes Works Cited)

Books:

Bagley, Laurie. 2008. *Summit.* Mt. Shasta: BayTree Publishing.

Ban Breathnach, Sarah. 1995. *Simple Abundance.* New York: Grand Central Publishing.

Brassard, Sarah. 2018. *Inside.* Las Vegas: Lifestyle Entrepreneurs Press.

Bhat, Nilima and Raj Sisodia. 2016. *Shakti Leadership.* Oakland: Berrett-Koehler Publishers. Inc.

Bhajan, Yogi. 1977. *The Teachings of Yogi Bhajan.* Santa Cruz: KRI Publications.

Blake, Trevor. 2012. *Three Simple Steps*. Dallas: BenBella Books. Inc.

Brene, Brown. *Daring Greatly*. 2012. New York: Penguin Random House.

Burchard, Brendon. 2017. *High Performance Habits*. Carlsbad: Hay House.

Campbell, Joseph. *The Hero's Journey*. 1990. New York: HarperCollins.

Canfield, Jack. 2005 2015. *The Success Principles*. New York: William Morrow.

Chacour, Elias with David Hazard. 1984. *Blood Brothers*. Grand Rapids: Baker Books.

Chapman, Gary. 1992. *The 5 Love Languages*. Chicago: Northfield Publishing.

Chödrön, Pema. 1996. *When Things Fall Apart*. Boston: Shambhala Publications, Inc.

Coelho, Paulo. 1998. *The Alchemist*. New York: Harper Collins Publishers.

Covey, Stephen. 1989. *The 7 Habits of Highly Effective People*. New York: Simon & Schuster. Inc.

Desai, Penache. 2014. *Discovering Your Soul Signature*. New York. Spiegel & Grau, Random House LLC.

Dyer, Wayne. 2015. *I Can See Clearly Now.* Carlsbad: Hay House.

Farrell, Warren; Gray, John. 2018. *The Boy Crisis.* Dallas: BenBella Books. Inc.

Frazier, Jan. 2007. *When Fear Falls Away.* San Francisco: CA / Newburyport, MA: Weiser Books.

Garr, Lisa. 2015. *Becoming Aware.* Carlsbad: Hay House.

Godin, Seth. 2008. *Tribes.* New York: Penguin Group Inc.

Gray, John. 2017. *Beyond Mars and Venus.* Dallas: BenBella Books, Inc.

Grout, Pam. 2013. *E Squared.* Carlsbad: Hay House.

Halaway, Dale. 2017. *Being Called to Change.* Las Vegas: Lifestyle Entrepreneur Press.

Hawkins, David. 2012. *Letting Go.* Carlsbad: Hay House.

Hendrix, Harville. 1988. *Getting the Love You Want.* New York: Holt Paperbacks.

Hesse, Herman. 1951. *Siddhartha.* New York: New Directions Publishing Corporation.

Holub, Ana. 2014. *Forgive and Be Free.* Woodbury: Llewellyn Worldwide.

Katie, Byron. 2002. *Loving What Is.* New York: Harmony Books.

Lipton, Bruce. 2005. *The Biology of Belief: Unleashing the Power of Consciousness, Matter, and Miracles.* Self-published; re-released with Hay House.

Lakhiani, Vishen. 2016. *The Code of the Extraordinary Mind.* Emmaus: Rodale Books.

Masters, Robert. 2018. *Bringing Your Shadow Out of the Dark.* Louisville: Sounds True.

Morter, Dr. Sue. 2019. *The Energy Codes.* New York: Atria Books.

Mt. Shasta, Peter. 2010. *Adventures of a Western Mystic.* Mount Shasta: Church of the Seven Rays.

Redfield, James. 1993. *The Celestine Prophecy.* New York: Hachette Book Group.

Rumi, Jalal al-Din. (1997) 2004. *The Essential Rumi.* Translated by Coleman Barks. New York: Penguin Books.

Shimoff, Marci. 2008. *Happy for No Reason.* New York: Simon & Schuster.

Singh, Guru. 2014. *Buried Treasures.* ReVolution Books.

Singer, Michael. 2007. *The Untethered Soul.* Louisville: Sounds True.

Tamura, Michael. 2002. *You Are the Answer*. Mt. Shasta: Star of Peace Publishing.

Tolle, Eckhart. 1999. *The Power of Now*. Novato: Namaste Publishing and New World Library.

Twist, Lynne. 2003. *The Soul of Money*. New York: W.W. Norton & Company.

Vanzant, Iyalnla. 2018. *Get Over It!: Thought Therapy for Healing the Hard Stuff*. Carlsbad: Hay House.

Williamson, Marianne. 2012. *The Law of Divine Compensation*. San Francisco: Harper One.

White, David. 2018. *The Bell and The Blackbird*. Langley: Many Rivers Press.

Zukav, Gary. 1989. *Seat of the Soul*. New York: Simon & Schuster.

Musicians:

Alanis Morissette
Deva Premal and Mitten
Diane Bardwell
India.Arie
Jana Stanfield
Karen Drucker

Kathy Zavada
Kelly Corsino
Olivia Newton-John
Peter Makena
Rickie Byars Beckwith

Acknowledgements

Beloved Kirk, you are my inspiration. You nudge me to balance and encourage my softening. Your understanding gives me the levity to see a higher path. As my companion in awakening and intimacy, I adore you. Your generous admiration shows me I am enough, as is. Thank you for believing in this book, reading rough drafts, and reminding me to be humble.

To my editor, Sylvia Somerville, you are an extraordinary companion in making sense of many organic, random, creative thoughts. Your ability to cherry-pick and restructure the manuscript "rocked my world." As a sincere spiritual aspirant, you brought sparkles of wisdom and power to every page. Thanks for seeing this through to the end.

Dear family and friends, the ones who saw me shake in my boots and told me to walk ahead anyway, the courage to express my art is fueled by your belief. Specifically, Mom Judy, Dad Marlyn, Sister Aria, Stephanie, Mary, Abraham, Justi, Laurie, Jeannie, Deborah, Sarah, Warren, Liz, Bill, Joann, and Shanti. Special thanks to those of you who also served as Beta Readers!

Thank you clients, and colleagues who shouted, "YES!" and gave comments when I posted an excerpt or book research questions on Facebook.

Thank you, Marci Shimoff, for suggesting the name of the book, *Inspired,* and for writing the Foreword. Brava, brilliant woman! Your cheerleading me to the finish line brightened my way.

Heartfelt appreciation goes to David Hazzard, my initial writing coach, who showed up as "The Remover of all Obstacles" when I doubted, postponed, got stuck, and wanted to give up.

You are patient, profoundly intelligent, and convincing. Thanks for lighting the fire called, *Inspired.*

To the publishing team at L.E. Press, you do put your authors first as you roll up your sleeves with commitment. You walked the author's path with me as powerful guides. Thank you, Michael Ireland, for seeing two books in one manuscript and for offering ideas, encouragement, and edits.

To David, my root spiritual teacher, you know who you are. The vibrancy of truth that flows through you—in stories, in messages, and in your compassionate ways—lives in every bit of wisdom in this book.

In appreciation for all the life opportunities and the people who trigger my growth, I give thanks. To my many Wisdom Warriors and way-showers, thank you for proving to me that angels do walk upon the Earth. To my "petty tyrants" who push my panic buttons and tempt me to detour, you played your parts well. In the afterview, I will see you as some of my greatest and most loving teachers.

About the Author

Joy Taylor is the founder of A Soul Inspired Life and past Director of the Women's Business Center in Northern California. Her passion is empowering individuals to make choices from soul inspired intentions, not personality-driven motivations. She defines success as living in alignment with your values—and that you choose success. In her consulting and training she is known as an "Intuitive Business Muse" and offers practical strategies and solutions to assist you in designing an authentic life and creating a purposeful and rewarding business.

Often called a truth-teller, Joy brings honesty and clarity to her programs, which currently include The Codes to Confidence Course, Your Soul Inspired Business Launch, and The Brave and Brilliant You Mentorship. Voted "MOST INSPIRATIONAL" in junior high and high school, it is her nature to inspire.

As an empathic and articulate professional, her compassion supports others to nurture their highest potential. Working with entrepreneurs, women leaders, and positive agents of change, Joy encourages you to embrace a learner mindset, live as a student of life, and give thanks for this journey of continual "becoming." Joy loves to help individuals break through inner obstacles, build confidence, and bring their visions to life.

Joy's first career was that of a somatic practitioner with a focus on Jin Shin Jyutsu˙, Reiki, and myo-fascial release techniques. Joy infused her practice with a variety of bodywork skills, heart-centered esoteric arts, and her Priestess initiation. She feels that her commitment to be a clear "vessel of healing" allowed for deep transformation (sometimes with miraculous results) for clients. Joy went on to be an Ambassador of The Amazon Herb Company. She dedicated a decade to a two-fold mission of health and rainforest preservation. In that role, she educated and led a large international sales team. It was through these experiences that Joy found her "sweet spot" as a trainer and consultant in conscious business and feminine leadership. Since 2001, she has helped thousands of people start and grow their business.

As an Artist, Healer, Teacher archetype, Joy continues to weave vitality, creativity, and loving energy into her professional development company.

After twenty years living at the base of sacred Mount Shasta in Northern California, Joy now resides with her Beloved Kirk, in Ashland, Oregon, where they enjoy nature, music, a healthy lifestyle, good company, and spiritual partnership.

Lisa Garr Interview with the Author

Interviewed by Lisa Garr, Creator of *The Aware Show* and #1 Amazon best-selling author of *Becoming Aware*. Learn more about Lisa's show at: *www.TheAwareShow.com*

Lisa Garr: **Joy, what inspires you to do what you do?**

Joy Taylor: You! And the Wisdom Warriors out there, sharing love.

Mostly, I am inspired when I feel a connection with life—with people, nature, and music.

I am also inspired by the human transformation that we are all making right now—the shift from personality-driven motivations to soul inspired intentions. I believe that humanity is becoming more soulful. On a global level, consciousness is moving towards love. This transformation inspires me because with this change, people are giving up their defenses and living in humility. I'm inspired by poetry, too. It is a soul language.

Lisa: **You write poetry and include it in your book, yes?**

Joy: Yes...and here is a good poem that answers your first question about what inspires me...

Can I now remember?
Sunlight on fresh snow nurtures my soul.
You see, what sings to me is beauty and nature,
The delicacy of words spoken from the core.
What excites me is a fresh moment,
Two adults laughing like children,
A poet sharing her work.
What moves me is a human being willing to be vulnerable.
What inspires me is some heroine living in the unknown.

Lisa: **What is the book about, in your own words?**

The book is about *becoming* the person you were born to be. I believe we are all born to be beautiful, unique, and great. We are all *becoming* in the ways that inspire us, and no one can prescribe that inspiration for us. We are on a never-ending journey of *becoming* our most natural, authentic self. I hope the book offers clear guidance for fellow travelers on that quest.

Lisa: **How does someone live the life they're meant to lead?**

Joy: I believe that evolving into our potential is a natural thing, but our personal challenges interfere. I say it is natural because the seed of potential for each and every one of us grows when we nurture it. The seed is our soul signature, the essence of who we are and the gifts and talents we have. Our job is to create a loving environment for our potential to blossom.

What interferes with that growth are the fearful parts of us, our programs from childhood, and our unconscious shadow. So, the real work is observing and challenging what holds us back, while noticing and serving the love that propels us forward.

Lisa: **How do people find their purpose?**

Joy: I believe we all have multiple purposes—not just one big 'life purpose.' Too many people get caught up in finding their 'life purpose' and lose track of all the many daily ways they can be purposeful. This 'life purpose' concept causes undue pressure and insecurity for a lot people.

I say, 'Relax, you are living your purpose when you show up in each moment with love.'

Basically, we are all here to *experience*, to *grow*, and to *give*. How you choose to do that is up to you.

The more you allow yourself to be the natural self that you are, the more your multiple purposes will show up for you. You will move forward to where you are drawn. You will feel pulled toward your purposes when you do little things every day that inspire you. Follow your inspirations and you find your purposes in life.

Lisa: **How did you develop the 7 Wisdoms?**

Joy: They first came to me after a contemplative prayer. I was doing what I usually do in the mornings;

taking quiet time to meditate, pray, journal, and having a cup of coffee. And on this particular morning, I heard a very distinct voice that said, "Life is for you."

I was struck by the presence and the energy of that voice. It was very calming. I made a note on my iPhone. Then I heard the next message, "You deserve it. You deserve love."

I took the messages in and then I thought, 'So, if I am living in a Benevolent Universe and I deserve all the good coming my way, I'm going to pay attention to life's cues. I want to have a conversation with this Benevolent Universe so I can receive all the blessings.'

After the first three messages, the next four Wisdoms came at once, and I took notes.

While the initial 'download' was about four minutes, developing the Wisdoms happened over many years of integrating them into my own life and utilizing them in my courses and consulting. My clients and I experimented with them and found that they really work. If you work on the Wisdoms, they will work on you.

Lisa: **Why did you write the book?**

Joy: In the process of writing the book, I asked myself that question all the time, "Oh my Goddess, why did I sign up for this?"

Writing this book was super challenging. It stretched me. I walked through fire as I wrote, rewrote, edited, and reviewed the manuscript. I tested the ideas and became a student of the words. It was grueling at times.

On one level, I wrote the book for my own transformation. It clarified so much for me in terms of knowing what I know and finding out how much I really don't know. Writing this book was scary and humbling. It brought me to my knees. I had to face my fears of not being a 'good-enough' writer. And now I am facing my fears of bad reviews and disapproval (another expression of the 'not-good-enough' tape).

However, the initial impetus for writing *Inspired* came from my belief that humanity is undergoing a great change. The old models of gain and manipulation are outdated and painful. I wrote in order to share with others that life is not about acquiring things. It's about receiving. It's not about making things happen, it's a about allowing things to happen. I wrote to introduce people to a new model of living.

I know that some people are feeling confused in this global transformation. The book is an offering to help people make sense of the changes and challenges they are going through. As people are questioning the status quo and the traditional ways we measure success, they need alternatives and applications. They need companion guides and mentors. I include a lot of quotes from other Wisdom Warriors to illustrate this collective movement towards a new Earth.

Because I am a practical person, I wrote a book that was not all philosophy, but actually full of tips and tools that people can utilize right away, which is why I have the 'Walk with the Wisdom' sections, the Guidebook, and online courses. I want people to take this information and use it!

Lisa: **Which Wisdom is most challenging for you?**

Joy: Wisdom Two – You Deserve Love.

I wrote and rewrote that chapter until my publisher told me, "Enough. We have a deadline." Writing about self-compassion was difficult for me. I got triggered by my own fears around not being loveable. Wisdom Two is full of both personal zingers and warm fuzzies.

Lisa: **Which Wisdom comes easiest for you?**

Joy: Both Wisdoms Six and Seven are the most natural for me. Gratitude and Giving are like cherries on the top of the Wisdom sundae. They are the organic outpourings of a soul inspired life. Besides, it is super fun to be grateful and I enjoy giving to others.

Lisa: **What did you learn in writing the book?**

Joy: I learned a lot! I learned how to fumble, fall, and find my balance again. I learned that writing a book is tedious, meticulous, time-consuming, and ultimately, a labor of love.

But the biggest lesson I learned (and gift) is humility. I had to let go of all my personality desires to 'prove myself' or to 'get recognition' from the book. I had to let go of 'protecting my reputation' and 'being liked.' I learned that I'm 'good enough' when I choose that I'm good enough. And, I am still learning all of this.

I read a quote from Joan of Arc. She said, 'I'm not afraid...I was born for this.' The more I realized I was born to practice and share this message, the less fear I felt. There are moments when we all shake in our boots and have butterflies in our stomachs. If we simply stay the course and come from our heart, we cannot lose, we can only give and grow.

Lisa: **What is your hope for the reader?**

Joy: I hope that readers experiment and study the Wisdoms in all areas of their lives, from career to relationships to health. I don't expect or want anyone to take my word for it. I encourage people to try on the Wisdoms for themselves. With courage, people can challenge stagnation and get into a flow state.

I hope people are gentle with themselves in the process. I hope that readers feel uplifted and go out and do good work in the world.

Lisa: **What is your biggest *why* — the biggest reason you do what you do?**

Joy: Love. Giving and receiving love (and inviting others to do the same). This is how we change the tides for a greater good.

It is what I see you doing, Lisa. Not everyone follows their passions like you do. I know it takes a lot of work to put on and publish your interviews and programs. Watching you over the years has really inspired me. Thank you.

I also want to thank everyone who is reading this interview (and the book). Any interest in *Inspired* signifies the desire to evolve, and evolving takes bravery. So, I applaud all you brave and brilliant people out there. Yes, that is YOU! Thank you.

Walking the Wisdoms with Joy

You are doing it. You are "walking the wisdoms" and taking action along your path of inspiration.

Welcome! You belong here.

There is no end to the path (that's good news), and there are many soul inspired friends awaiting your contributions and eager to support you. You are not alone.

What I've found (and shared in *Inspired*) is that "good company" offers guidance, connection, and direction. We propel each other forward with grace and compassion. Together, we grow. Together, we achieve. Together, we are love in action. You belong with us. Join us.

Below are some ways you can continue to Walk the Wisdoms with Joy!

A Soul Inspired Life Online

www.ASoulInspiredLife.com is the hub!

Great resources await you, including the "Wisdom Activations" and other gifts. You'll find a program schedule and invitations to grow.

Join the mailing list for special discounts and opportunities, as well as useful, proven, and effective insights and inspirations to become your most authentic self and turn your passions into your purpose.

Subscribe to my YouTube Channel (JoyTaylorInspired) as I "Talk Inspiration." Watch truth-telling interviews with "Wisdom

Warriors," plus pick up relevant and practical tools for soul inspired entrepreneurs, leaders, and courageous creators, like you.

Programs and Services

I love facilitating personal and professional breakthroughs.

Online Group Programs

The Codes to Confidence Course:
Give yourself the gift of 7 weeks to actualize a more bold, brave, and brilliant you. Bring out the best in yourself while enjoying a natural connection, momentum, and congruence with your soul signature. Very interactive in nature, join this safe and supportive environment as you understand and apply the codes to confidence. You'll be introduced to revolutionary skills that can become real game changers in how you live, love, and lead.

Your Soul Inspired Business:
Are you ready to launch a dream business? This program is based on proven entrepreneurial methods for starting and growing business, but with a little twist—everything is designed from the inside out. Create your products with your customer journey in mind. Clarify your message and infuse it with love (not fear). Develop compelling outreach and leave manipulation behind. Organize your business to avoid overwhelm. Find success utilizing the "ultimate-leverage" intuition.

Inspired Action Groups:
Much like a mastermind, you'll accelerate your projects in the presence of other soul inspired business owners and leaders. With powerful activations and benevolent energetics, I facilitate inspiration in action. These groups are limited in size to allow

for real-time business decisions and conscious choice points. You'll be amazed to see your professional intentions take flight, your creativity soar, and your personal power elevate.

In-person Retreats:
Here is your opportunity to be in the presence of a collective brilliance. Take the time to renew yourself, make new friends, and evolve. You'll be encouraged to take what you've learned in *Inspired* and go deeper. You'll explore your own inner knowing and experience breakthroughs. (You know how it is! Inspiration is creative and every live event is unique based on who attends.)

Private Consulting and Intensives:
If you are ready for big shifts in your life or career, let me be your business intuitive muse.

Inspirational Speaking:
For group presentations, guest webinars, or media interviews, see my signature talks and media sheet online.

Be a Wisdom Warrior

Start a Study Group
When you purchase *The Inspired Guidebook,* you'll learn more about creating small groups where you can share in discussions and activities to embody the Wisdoms. Join together and go through the book and guidebook in the company of like-minded and soul inspired friends.

Did this book change you?
I want to hear about your insights and "aha moments." Let me know what part of the book resonated with you and where you are on the path. When you review the book online, leave your

inspiration for others. This is how we encourage a more soul inspired planet.

Where are you inspired?
Post a photo of you with Inspired. Show us where you are reading it. Are you by the fireside, on the beach, with your cat, or having a cup of coffee? Maybe you are on a train in Europe or sitting on a mountain top. I want to know! Where are you *inspired*? Be creative and post on social media with: *#SoulInspired #IamInspired*

Tag me *@JoyTaylorInspired* on Instagram or Facebook

Live, love, and lead your soul inspired life.

9 781948 787178

Praise for Joy Taylor and *Inspired*

"This book is a timely antidote to the growing sense of fear that we live in an unsafe world."

~ **John Gray**, New York Times best-selling author of *Men Are from Mars, Women Are from Venus*

"*Inspired* offers a refreshing and modern-day take on personal development. Apply the Wisdoms and your life will improve."

~ **Jack Canfield**, co-author of the *Chicken Soup for the Soul®* series and *The Success Principles*™

"If you're ready to embrace a deeply meaningful and love-filled life, this book is your golden ticket."

~ **Marci Shimoff**, New York Times best-selling author of *Happy for No Reason*

"Humanity is now awakening to our true essence and releasing the confinement of living from our limited personalities alone. *Inspired*, with its user-friendly guidance of deep soulful wisdom and reference to today's relevant science, helps us merge into our greatness and live a life uncommon. It's the perfect operator's manual for today's transformational seeker!"

~ **Dr. Sue Morter**, founder of *Morter Institute for BioEnergetics*, author of *The Energy Codes*

"If you want to get Inspired to re-choose your dream or discover your dream, this is a perfect book to enlighten your soul to live an Inspired life!"

~ **Lisa Garr**, host and creator of *The Aware Show*

"Joy's words and spirit exude possibility. You don't just hear inspiration; you feel inspired."

~ **Dr. Warren Farrell**, author of *The Boy Crisis*

"Inspired is a joy to read. It is like breathing inspiration on every page right into your heart!"

~ **Nicola Amadora, PhD**, Psychologist, Spiritual Teacher, founder of *Living Connection*

"This is truly a soul-inspired book that couldn't come at a better time. The very survival of humankind is on the line and we need the guidance and support that Joy so beautifully offers. The book is a must read for men and women who are ready to make a difference in the world."

~ **Jed Diamond, PhD**, international best-selling author of *The Irritable Male Syndrome*

"Comforting in the best sense of the word, as in, helping us become present 'with strength,' every page of Joy Clarissa Taylor's *Inspired* lives up to the promise of its title and shares the blessings of radiant soul-inspiration with us all. Joy has a talent for communicating profound truths in language that is simple and directly accessible, yet not at all simplistic. If your soul thirsts, here is an inexhaustible well of '7 Wisdoms.' Drink deep!"

~ **Saniel Bonder**, author of *Healing the Spirit/ Matter Split*, founder of *Waking Down*®

"If you're looking for direction and inspiration, this is the book for you."

~ **Kamala Chambers**, author of *Road To Love*, founder of *ThrivingLaunch.com*